WAGE INCENTIVES
as a Managerial Tool

WAGE INCENTIVES

as a Managerial Tool

by WILLIAM B. WOLF

1957

Columbia University Press, New York

To Nancy, Pete, and Steve

Preface

This is a study of the use of wage incentives in manufacturing plants. It was originally started in 1944. At that time I was in charge of the standards department of a relatively large company. In comparing my experience in administering wage incentives with the reports appearing in the current literature I noticed significant discrepancies between expectations and results. Furthermore, talks with fellow practitioners failed to provide a logical framework for viewing wage incentives. Thus this study was started in order to discover the sense and/or non-sense of using wage incentives to remunerate rank-and-file factory workers. The particular contribution which it purports to make is to give both the student and the practitioner a fuller understanding of the use of this technique.

In the preparation of this book I am deeply indebted to many businessmen and union leaders. They gave patiently of their time and knowledge to supply much of the data in this book. However, for obvious reasons they must remain anonymous. A number of my colleagues have given helpful suggestions, especially Professors William Vatter, Raleigh W. Stone, Robert K. Burns, and Ezra Solomon, of the University of Chicago, and Professors Cornelius Gillam and Robert A. Sutermeister, of the University of Washington. In addition, the support of Dean Austin Grimshaw of the College of Business Administration of the University of Washington has done much to make this book a reality.

WILLIAM B. WOLF

The College of Business Administration
The University of Washington
Seattle, Washington
October, 1956

Contents

WAGE INCENTIVES
as a Managerial Tool

I The Nature of
WAGE INCENTIVES

INTRODUCTION

In spite of the attention that the Scientific Management
Movement and the Second World War emergency focused
on the use of wage incentives, very little has been done to
analyze their implications for management.[1] In the management literature, most of the attention has been centered
on descriptions of specific wage incentive plans, discussion
of the ostensible benefits of specific plans, and mechanical
comparisons of the cost curves associated with various wage
incentive formulae.[2]

[1] One of the first tasks in the preparation of this study was to review the
existing literature on wage incentives. The review was made to determine
what had already been done and to provide a check for the findings of this
investigation.

Though the review revealed a vast amount of writing, most of it is from
a nonmanagement point of view. For example, it appears that Karl Marx
was one of the first writers to study the impact of wage incentives systematically. He analyzed early English experience as revealed by the official reports of the Inspectors of Factories and the Children's Employment Com-
mission. See *Capital* (Modern Library ed.; New York, Random House, Inc.,
1906), pp. 605–11. For other early comments on the use of wage incentives,
see Adam Smith, *Wealth of Nations* (Modern Library ed.; New York, Random House, Inc., 1937), Book I, Chap. VIII, p. 61; Sidney and Beatrice
Webb, *Industrial Democracy* (London, Longmans, Green and Co., 1902),
Chap. V.

The most thorough studies of wage incentives have dealt with union attitudes and activities. For example, the Webbs, *Industrial Democracy;*
David A. McCabe, "The Standard Rate in American Trade Unions," in
Johns Hopkins University Studies in Historical and Political Science (Balti-
more, The Johns Hopkins Press, 1912), Series XXI, No. 2; G. D. H. Cole,
The Payment of Wages (London, George Allen and Unwin, Ltd., 1918);
Sumner H. Slichter, *Union Policies and Industrial Management* (Wash-
ington, Brookings Institution, 1941), Chaps. X and XI; Van Dusen Ken-
nedy, *Union Policy and Incentive Wage Methods* (New York, Columbia
University Press, 1945).

[2] Most of the management literature appears in periodicals. Very few
books on wage incentives per se have been written. Those that do devote

An analysis of the classic book on the subject (Charles W. Lytle's *Wage Incentive Methods*) reveals scarcely a paragraph indicating the concepts underlying the use of wage incentives or the multiple complications arising from their use.

This concentration on specific techniques and practices has lost sight of the general problem and has failed to induce formulation of the major concepts necessary for a proper perspective on the subject. It needs to be supplemented by an empirical study of the actual impact of wage incentives and an analysis of how these findings compare with the logic underlying their use. Such an analysis is necessary to provide both the student and the practitioner with a concise set of principles for dealing with wage incentives in their true perspective.

This study is designed to provide such an analysis. Chapter II describes the impact of wage incentives as revealed by field investigations, Chapter III analyzes the logic of wage incentives, and Chapter IV sets forth precepts and caveats to guide those concerned with the use of wage incentives.

Before the impact of wage incentives can be described, attention must be given to the definition of the term and to the nature of the use of this device. Accordingly, the present chapter discusses the definition of wage incentives, their use as a management technique, and the history of

---

considerable attention to wage incentives are essentially descriptive and nontheoretical. For example: David F. Schloss, *Methods of Industrial Remuneration* (Oxford, England, Williams and Norgate, 3d ed. 1898); Daniel Bloomfield, *Financial Incentives for Employees and Executives* (New York, The H. W. Wilson Co., 1923), Vol. I.; L. P. Alford, ed., *Management's Handbook* (New York, Ronald Press Co., 1924), Sec. 16.; Charles W. Lytle, *Wage Incentive Methods* (rev. ed.; New York, Ronald Press Co., 1938); Hugo Diemer, ed., *Wage-Payment Plans That Reduce Production Costs* (New York, McGraw-Hill Publishing Co., Inc., 1929); Carl C. Harrington, ed., *Job Evaluation and Wage Incentives* (New York, Conover-Mast Publications, Inc., 1949); Norman C. Hunt, *Methods of Wage Payment in British Industry* (London, Sir Isaac Pitman and Sons, Ltd., 1951).

their development. It concludes with a brief description of some of the more common wage incentive plans.

DEFINITION OF WAGE INCENTIVES

As used in this study, the term "wage incentives" refers to systems of remunerating rank-and-file workers under which the earnings of a worker, or a group of workers, are directly, promptly, and automatically related to his output by a predetermined formula relating his actual performance to a specific standard of performance. The essential characteristics of wage incentives are: (1) a standard of performance for each job or task is specifically established; and (2) the worker's earnings are directly, promptly, and automatically varied according to an established formula for relating actual performance to the standard.

Wage incentives are to be differentiated from time wages.[3] Under the latter method of wage payment, the worker is paid on the basis of the time he works rather than according to his output. This difference is essentially one of degree.[4] In a time wage system, standards of output are usually implied, and frequently the worker's hourly wage rate reflects the level of his efficiency. However, the standard of output is implicit rather than explicit, and the relationship between earnings and output is not definite, automatic, or immediate.

Frequently time wages and wage incentives are combined within a single wage payment system. Workers may

[3] In the literature there is a great deal of confusion in terminology. What is referred to above as "time wages" is also sometimes called "day work," "time work," or "straight-time."

[4] The line of demarcation between wage incentives and time wages is faint. For example: Under a measured day rate system, explicit standards of performance are determined. However, if no definite and precise relationship between remuneration and output is established, the system is not technically a wage incentive. If there is a definite and precise method for promptly relating the worker's output to his earnings, the system is classified as a wage incentive.

be given a guaranteed minimum rate of earnings per hour and then be paid a bonus [5] or premium for all production in excess of the established standard of output. Such combinations are classified as wage incentives because the level of incentive earnings is usually considerably above the hourly guaranteed wage rate, and the characteristics of wage incentives are present (that is, explicit standards of performance are set, and, within limits, the relationship between output and earnings is definite, immediate, and automatic).

WAGE INCENTIVES AS A MANAGERIAL TOOL

Wage incentives are a managerial tool. Their primary purpose is to aid in obtaining minimum unit costs, thereby contributing to enterprise profits. Lytle says that "the primary and universal reason for the installation of wage payment plans (i.e., wage incentives) is today, as ever, to secure the lowering of unit costs on the one hand, and to improve the earnings of the employees on the other." [6] The manner in which wage incentives reduce costs has been described in terms of numerous intermediate objectives. For example, a representative of the Westinghouse Electric Elevator Company stated that the objectives and anticipated results of a scientifically worked out wage incentive plan are:

1. Production problems or maladjustments are brought to immediate attention due to a drop in the incentive bonus factor.

2. Better segregation of efficient workers thus insuring a full utilization of available manpower.

3. Better planning of details of the job and also the methods of the job by supervisors or industrial engineers.

---

[5] As used in this study, the term "bonus" refers to earnings in excess of the worker's guaranteed hourly wage rate.

[6] Lytle, *Wage Incentive Methods,* p. 53.

4. Increase in production due to the accumulation of the above benefits plus the major factor of increased effort on the part of the operator.

5. Better morale of the worker whenever the plan is administered efficiently and fairly.

    a. Because of his effort, he can increase his earnings.

    b. By his production, he can gauge his own merit and work.

    c. By seeing immediate return for efforts expended, he applies himself to his task willingly and cheerfully.[7]

Riegel [8] lists several slightly different benefits which result from the use of wage incentives:

1. Greater output per hour on each job on incentive brought about lower unit costs for direct labor and overhead.

2. Accurate predetermination of costs—essential in mass production industries which contract for production in advance—was made possible.

3. Unit costs were stabilized while wage rates and prices of material remained constant.

4. The reduction of watching and bossing to obtain employee application on the job had some favorable influence on industrial relations.

5. The production standards, which are apart from but essential to an incentive plan, were helpful in planning, scheduling, and coordinating production, and in forecasting equipment and manpower needs.

Lionel Michael enumerates the following advantages derived from "a sound wage incentive plan, properly conceived, installed and administered": [9]

1. More effective operation through standardization of methods and costs.

---

[7] *Experience of 123 Companies with Wage Incentive Plans, Section I* (Chicago, Dartnell Corporation, 1944), p. 12.

[8] John W. Riegel, "Essentials in Incentive Compensation," in *Developments in Wage Payment Techniques,* American Management Association Personnel Series, No. 77 (1944), p. 12.

[9] Lionel B. Michael, *Wage and Salary Fundamentals and Procedures* (New York, McGraw-Hill, 1950), pp. 235–36.

2. Increased production through improved methods and greater worker productivity.

3. Reduction of unit costs through greater utilization of equipment and worker effort.

4. Increased market potentialities through providing a product at an attractive price.

In summary, wage incentives are essentially a managerial tool for reducing cost. In achieving this goal, two closely related areas are emphasized: (1) the role of wage incentives in motivating workers to increase their rate of output, and (2) the role of wage incentives in stimulating management to be more efficient in performing its functions. The impact of wage incentives is to be appraised in terms of their efficacy in achieving these ends. However, before considering the actual impact of wage incentives, it is desirable to reflect upon the history of their development and related matters, thus providing a more thorough and complete background for the analysis of their use.

THE DEVELOPMENT OF WAGE INCENTIVES

Wage incentives have a long history. They have existed since the inception of the employer-employee relationship.[10] Records show that the principal type of wage incentive—piece rate—was used in the ancient Egyptian, Roman, and Grecian economies.[11]

One of the early uses of wage incentives was under the home-work system of manufacturing. Under this form of organization wage incentive problems differed from those in modern manufacturing. The incentive aspect of the wage payment system was probably of secondary importance, since the employer was interested primarily in receiving a specified quantity of work for a given price. As long as an adequate supply of labor was available, he was

---

[10] The Webbs, *Industrial Democracy*, p. 285.
[11] Harlow S. Person, "Methods of Remuneration," in *Encyclopedia of the Social Sciences*, VIII (1935), 672–82.

under little pressure to be seriously concerned about the worker's rate of output.

The modern use of wage incentives is associated with the development of the factory system. With the centering of production in the factory the incentive aspect gained added importance, since the employer was now faced with the task of spreading his overhead by increasing output.

The rapid industrialization during the last half of the nineteenth century directed increased attention to the limitations of wage incentives.[12] It stimulated the search for some form of wage payment which would have incentive value yet still be free from rate cutting and restriction of output. This search led to innovations in wage incentive systems as well as to the consideration of various alternative means of motivating workers.[13]

The development of modern wage incentive plans followed two general approaches. The first was the development of systems wherein employer and employees would share the savings in direct labor costs resulting from increased production. The logic underlying these plans was that the sharing feature would eliminate management's need and desire to cut rates. The Halsey and Rowan plans are examples of this approach.[14] They provided for standards of output based on records of past performance, and

---

12 The point of emphasis was that workers' fear of rate cutting prompted them to restrict output.

13 Consideration of the alternatives to wage incentives is outside the scope of the present discussion. However, it is appropriate to point out that various forms of profit sharing and the use of nonfinancial incentives were suggested as solutions to the problems of rate cutting and restriction of output. See: Henry R. Towne, "Gain Sharing," in *Transactions of the American Society of Mechanical Engineers* (New York, 1889), Vol. X; Nicholas P. Gilman, *Profit Sharing between Employer and Employee* (New York, Houghton Mifflin and Co., 1889); R. B. Wolf, "Nonfinancial Incentives," in *Publications of the American Society of Mechanical Engineers* (1918), No. 1673, quoted in John R. Commons, ed., *Trade Unionism and Labor Problems* (New York, Ginn and Co., 1921), pp. 218–32.

14 F. A. Halsey, "The Premium Plan of Paying for Labor," in *Transactions of the American Society of Mechanical Engineers* (New York, 1891), Vol. XII; W. Rowan Thomson, *The Premium Bonus System* (Glasgow, Scotland, McCorquodale and Co., Ltd., 1917).

they paid workers only a part of the savings in direct labor cost arising from production in excess of the established standard. Since these plans provided a formula for relating wages to output in a manner that would eliminate the pressure for rate cutting, it was argued that they removed the main cause for restriction of output.

The second approach to the problem was a direct attack on the method of setting standards. The underlying reasoning was that setting correct standards of performance would automatically eliminate rate cutting and restriction of output. This logic was first popularized by F. W. Taylor.[15] His central theme is represented by the following quotation:

Since [under the Taylor system] the rate-fixing is done from accurate knowledge instead of more or less by guess-work, the motive for holding back on work, for 'soldiering' and endeavoring to deceive the employer as to the time required to do the work, is entirely removed, and with it the greatest cause for hard feelings and war between the management and the men.[16]

The procedure advocated by Taylor was "to resolve each job into its elements, to make a careful study of the quickest time in which each of the elementary operations can be done, and then to properly classify, tabulate, and index this information, and use it when required for rate fixing." [17]

WAGE INCENTIVE FORMULAE [18]

From 1891 to the 1920s, numerous formulae for relating earnings to output were developed. Some had unique fea-

[15] F. W. Taylor, "A Piece-Rate System," in *Transactions of the American Society of Mechanical Engineers* (New York, 1894 and 1895), XVI, 856–903.
[16] *Ibid.*, pp. 857–58.
[17] *Ibid.*, p. 869.
[18] Since this study is concerned with the more general aspects of wage incentives, only cursory attention is given to the specific formulae. For de-

tures; others were simply identical plans under different names. This section describes only a few of the better known plans. These are the piece rate plan, the standard hours plan, the Halsey Premium Plan, the Rowan Plan, the Bedaux Point Plan, the Taylor Differential Piece Rate Plan, the Merrick Multiple Piece Rate, the Gantt Task and Bonus System, and the Parkhurst Differential Bonus System.

Piece rate. The piece rate system is the oldest form of wage incentive. It provides for payment to workers at a constant price per unit of output. The worker's earnings are determined by multiplying his output by the price per unit.

Under most modern piece rate plans, a minimum hourly rate of pay is guaranteed to the worker. Hence, for low levels of output, the plan becomes a time wage plan.

Standard hours plan. The only significant difference between the standard hours plan and the piece rate plan is that for the former the standards of performance are quoted in units of time, rather than in money. Under a standard hours plan the worker is paid at his established hourly wage for all standard hours of work he produces, regardless of the time he actually takes to complete the work. For example, if a worker completes a job in four hours, and if six standard hours are allowed for that job, his earnings for the job will be six times his hourly rate of pay.

Halsey Premium Plan. The Halsey Premium Plan is closely related to the standard hours plan. In fact, one ver-

sion of the Halsey plan (the 100 percent premium plan) is
identical with the standard hours plan.[19] The more common version of the Halsey plan provides that employer
and employees share the savings in direct labor cost arising
from above-standard output. In the United States, the
exact percentage of the savings going to labor varies. The
most usual sharing is on a 50-50 basis.

An example will serve to illustrate the mechanics of the
Halsey 50-50 sharing plan. If six standard hours are allowed for a job and the worker actually performs the job
in four hours, his earnings are calculated as follows:

$$E = TR + (A - T)PR$$

Where E equals earnings, T equals time taken, A equals
time allowed, R equals the worker's hourly rate of pay,
and P equals the percentage of time saved paid to the
worker (in this case, 50 percent). In this example earnings
are equal to four times the worker's hourly rate of pay
plus his hourly rate times one-half of the time saved.

$$E = 4R + (6 - 4) \ .5R$$
$$E = 4R + R$$
$$E = 5R$$

As pointed out above, this plan was specifically designed
to reduce the need for rate cutting. Halsey reasoned that
allowing management to share directly in the savings of
direct labor cost mitigated management's need to cut rates
and so eliminated the main cause for restriction of output.

Rowan Plan. The Rowan Plan is similar to the Halsey
sharing plan in that it, too, provides a system whereby
management and labor may share the savings of direct

[19] It should be emphasized that this discussion is limited to the formulae
for relating earnings to output. As originally described by Halsey, his plan
was designed for use with loose standards of performance based on past
performance. As used in present-day industry this is not necessarily the
case. The Halsey plan often is used in connection with standards of output
determined by systematic time and motion study.

Nature of Wage Incentives

labor costs resulting from above-standard performance. The significant difference between the Halsey plan and the Rowan Plan is that under the former the sharing of savings between workers and employer is constant, whereas under the latter the workers receive a decreasing share of the savings as their rate of output increases. The reason for this is that under the Rowan Plan the worker's bonus is calculated as the percentage represented by time saved divided by time allowed. For example, if a worker receives $1.00 per hour and takes seven hours to do a job for which he is allowed ten hours, his earnings are calculated as follows:

$$E = TR + \left(\frac{A - T}{A}\right) TR$$

Where E equals earnings, T equals time taken, R equals rate of pay per hour, and A equals time allowed.

$$E = (\$1.00 \times 7) + [\frac{10 - 7}{10}(\$1.00 \times 7)]$$
$$E = \$9.10$$

In this example the bonus for saving three hours of time is $2.10 or 70 cents per hour. If the job is done in six hours, earnings will be $8.40, and the bonus will be $2.40 or 60 cents per hour. If the job is completed in zero time, the bonus is 100 percent of time taken, or zero. The merits of this plan arise from its self-limiting feature. With the Rowan formula for calculating bonus it is impossible for earnings to get too far out of line.

Bedaux Point Premium Plan. As originally designed, the Bedaux plan was identical to the Halsey 75-25 sharing plan. Recently the plan has been revised so that the workers receive 100 percent of time saved, and accordingly the present-day Bedaux formula is identical to the 100 percent premium version of the Halsey plan and the standard hours plan.

The unique features of the Bedaux plan are apparent

in the system of controls installed for administering the plan. Each job is reduced to a common denominator consisting of units of time required by an average worker working under normal conditions. These units are called "B's." Each "B" represents an average minute of working time. Usually, sixty "B's" per hour represents standard performance, and expected performance of experienced workers is around eighty "B's" per hour.[20]

Taylor Differential Piece Rate Plan. The Taylor Differential Piece Rate Plan differs from conventional piece rates in that the Taylor plan provides for two piece rates on each job. One piece rate is considerably higher than the going time wage for the job, and the other is somewhat below the time wage. The higher rate is paid only when workers attain or exceed a given level of performance. This level of performance is established by systematic time study. It is referred to in the literature as a "high task" standard (that is, it represents the rate of output which may be expected from an average skilled worker properly trained for the job and working at an incentive pace). Generally the "high task" standard is approximately 50 to 60 percent greater than the average rate of output maintained by the workers under a time wage system. The time wage level of output is referred to as "low task" output.

In establishing two piece rates for each job, Taylor hoped to motivate workers with a significant monetary reward for "high task" production and, at the same time, to discourage inefficient workers from remaining with the company.

Merrick Multiple Piece Rate Plan. In actual practice the Taylor Differential Piece Rate Plan did not work well. As soon as workers saw that they could not produce at a

---

[20] Several systems similar to the Bedaux plan are described in the literature. See the Haynes-Manit plan and the Dyer plan as discussed in Lytle, *Wage Incentive Methods,* pp. 246, 253–54.

"high task" level on a given job, they would slacken their pace. To overcome this weakness, Merrick added another piece rate to the differential plan. The first rate—the lowest price per piece—applies up to 83 percent of "high task"; from 83 percent to 100 percent of "high task" an intermediate piece rate price applies, and for higher levels of output the highest piece rate is paid.

Gantt Task and Bonus System. The Gantt Task and Bonus System was designed to remedy a problem similar to that which the Merrick plan attacked: the complications arising when workers failed to qualify for high piece rate. Gantt did this by guaranteeing hourly earnings and paying the equivalent of Taylor's high piece rate when workers produced at "high task" or above. In short, the Gantt plan provides a guaranteed hourly rate of pay for all work below the "high task" level. For all output above that level, the worker receives 100 percent of time saved plus a bonus of 20 percent of time saved. In this manner, Gantt attempted to overcome opposition encountered with the Differential Piece Rate Plan and to ease the burden on trainees and new employees.

Parkhurst Differential Bonus System. The Parkhurst bonus plan was designed to keep bonus or premium earnings separate and distinct from the employee's regular wages, and hence to avoid the difficulty of having bonus considered a part of wages instead of a reward for work well done.

Under the Parkhurst plan, bonus is a definite scale of dollars and cents established for different levels of efficiency on various classes of work. The types of work performed in the plant are separated into a number of classes. A specific job's classification is based on such criteria as the responsibility of the worker for machinery, the skill required to perform the job, and the physical effort involved in the work.

Bonus is determined by comparing actual output per unit of time with a standard established by time study. The time wage paid each employee is entirely separate from his bonus earnings and is even paid in a separate check.

In summary, there are numerous formulae for relating output to earnings. The unique features of many of these arose from specific operating problems. For example: the Halsey and Rowan formulae were designed to remove the fear of rate cutting; the Taylor Differential Piece Rate Plan was designed to force out the slower and less skilled worker; the Merrick and the Gantt plans attempted to mitigate the harshness of the Taylor Differential Piece Rate; and the Parkhurst attempted to maintain premium earnings as distinct and separate from normal hourly wages and thus to maintain the "bonus" characteristic of extra earnings.

From the point of view of this study, the differences between the formulae are relatively unimportant. They deal with minor modifications of the basic idea of wage incentives, and so are only incidental to analysis of the general nature of the impact of wage incentives.

II   The Impact of
WAGE INCENTIVES
on Manufacturing Costs

AN EMPIRICAL STUDY

INTRODUCTION

SCOPE AND METHOD OF THE EMPIRICAL INVESTIGATION

The preceding chapter described, in general terms, the nature of wage incentives. It pointed out that, as a management tool, their primary objective is to aid in obtaining minimum costs. The present chapter will analyze empirical evidence of their efficacy in attaining this goal. It will do so by describing the impact of wage incentives as observed in a number of case studies.

These case studies cover the use of wage incentives in remunerating rank-and-file workers employed on a tenure basis in manufacturing plants. Included in the study are plants manufacturing asbestos textiles, insulations, women's apparel, farm equipment, steel, metal containers, plumbing supplies, hospital supplies, cosmetics, diesel engines, paint, and ribbon.

It should be pointed out that the scope of this study has been limited. The use of wage incentives in remunerating salesmen, supervisors, and casual labor has been excluded. Furthermore, no attempt has been made to study the use of group incentive plans. These restrictions arise from the limitations of this writer's resources, and from the fact that the excluded materials pose special problems.

A further point that should be mentioned with respect

to the scope of this study is that the case situations investigated have been restricted to relatively well-managed
plants. It is felt that the study of such installations provides the most reliable background for judging the impact
of wage incentives on costs.

The twenty-six cases included in this study cover plants
employing from 100 to 17,000 rank-and-file workers. Most
of the plants employed 400 to 700 workers. Selection of
the cases was not governed by the size of the plant. It was
based on the availability of information, the nature of the
manufacturing processes in the plant, and the attention
given to administration of the wage incentive system.

The data on each case were secured by interviewing.
Where possible, this was supplemented by a review of the
written records of the company. More than 180 representatives of management, rank-and-file workers, and union
leaders were interviewed. From case to case there were
variations in the number of persons interviewed and the
number of follow-up interviews. For example: In one case
the writer's information came from six years of experience as a participant-observer. In another case information
was gathered by intermittent observations over a two-year
period. In the other cases data were gathered through less
extended studies. In most of the cases both supervisors and
workers were interviewed; however, in a few cases it was
possible to contact only supervisors, and in several other
cases data were gathered solely through interviews with
workers.

With few exceptions, information was obtained by
friendly and informal interviews. The writer was fortu-
nate in having an opportunity to conduct a series of courses
on wage and salary administration for the officers of a
number of local unions. The rapport established in this
relationship helped greatly in obtaining confidential and
frank descriptions of how wage incentives affected the ac-

tivities of rank-and-file workers. Another factor contributing to depth of analysis was the fact that executives from several of the companies included in this investigation were students in graduate courses taught by this writer. Their sincere cooperation was most helpful in providing data that normally would have been difficult to obtain.

CHARACTER OF THE FINDINGS

To interpret properly the findings of the empirical part of this study it is first necessary to consider some of the limiting factors. It should be pointed out that only twenty-six cases were investigated. This raises questions as to the representativeness of the findings. Although analysis of additional cases would have been helpful, it is felt that the number and types covered are adequate for the purpose of this study. The cases cover a variety of industrial plants; further, the case findings were checked against the existing literature, and, most important, they have been tested by analytical reasoning. Thus, the empirical part of this study, when considered in the light of the other aspects of the study, is sufficiently inclusive to serve as a guide to understanding the general impacts of wage incentives.

Another type of limitation in the data of this study arises from weaknesses inherent in the interview method. The raw data supplied by field interviews consist of descriptions, attitudes, and opinions. These are frequently confusing and contradictory. Often informants fail to differentiate "what is" from "what they believe" and "what they desire." Thus, information gained through field interviews has to be weighed carefully to separate facts from beliefs and value judgments. There are further limitations encountered in studying case situations by the interview method. Most people are ignorant of many aspects of their immediate work environment, and are not fully aware of their own motivations. Thus the interview material tends to be weakened by the prejudices and ignorance of informants.

In the course of this investigation a conscious attempt has been made to mitigate these weaknesses in the interview method. Information has been carefully sifted and weighed. Wherever possible it has been checked against written records. Furthermore, attention has been focused on the activities of those interviewed, rather than on their unsupported opinions and attitudes.

PRESENTATION OF THE FINDINGS

Not only do the scope and method of this investigation establish limitations on its results, but the nature of the subject matter limits the way in which these results can be presented. Wage incentives exist in a system of complex casual relations, and they are used under a variety of conditions. Consequently, it is doubtful whether conclusions of universal applicability may be drawn. However some generalization is possible, for regardless of the conditions under which wage incentives are used, their principal problems are the same. They involve setting and maintaining standards of performance and an "equitable" wage structure. In dealing with these, certain common principles can be developed.

Since this investigation is concerned primarily with the general impact of wage incentives, the materials have been selected to illustrate the more common activities and events associated with their use. In this manner the prevailing effects of wage incentives are brought together in an organized fashion, and logical inference as to their contribution to low-cost production is facilitated.[1]

1 No attempt has been made to calculate the impact of wage incentives in dollars and cents. This follows from inherent weaknesses in the use of cost data: Unit cost is seldom clearly definable, and is not always susceptible to precise calculation. Unit costs are affected by many things in addition

For purpose of discussion the materials are organized under the following headings: (1) the effect of wage incentives on the general level of plant wages, (2) the operating problems associated with the use of wage incentives, (3) management activities associated with the administration of wage incentives, and (4) an evaluation of the impact of wage incentives on costs.

The Effect of Wage Incentives on the General Level of Plant Wages

Wage incentives have two important impacts on wages. One involves the structure of earnings within the firm. The other concerns the relationship of the general level of plant wages under an incentive system to that found under a time wage system. The present discussion is concerned with the latter of these impacts.[2]

Statistical evidence indicates that workers paid under a wage incentive system generally earn more per hour than they would under a time wage system. Two types of studies support this statement. One shows the increase in earnings associated with changing from time wages to a wage incentives system. The other compares incentive earnings with time wage earnings on similar jobs.

In 1943, the Bureau of Labor Statistics of the U.S. Department of Labor compared the hourly earnings of time workers with those of incentive workers in identical occupations. Three important industries were covered by this investigation: machinery manufacture, cotton-textile

---

to wage incentives. They may change due to variations in lot size, changes in machinery, changes in management efficiency, etc. In the absence of a means for precisely measuring the impact of wage incentives, this writer has observed their operation and proceeded, on the basis of logical reasoning, to infer their impact.

[2] For a consideration of the impact of wage incentives on the internal wage structure of the plant, see pp. 30–32.

manufacture, and primary fabrication of nonferrous metals. The study revealed

a definite and substantial margin in favor of the workers paid under incentive plans. . . . In roughly half of the occupations in which comparisons were made, incentive workers were earning, per hour, between 10 and 20 per cent more than the time workers. Differences of less than 5 per cent or more than 30 per cent were but rarely encountered and appeared, in most cases, to reflect deficiencies in the statistical data available for analysis.[3]

The general nature of these findings is supported by a later study conducted during 1945 and 1946. This study is based on a survey of 34,000 manufacturing establishments with about five and one-half million workers, and 21,000 nonmanufacturing establishments with about one and one-half million workers. It concludes:

Generally, incentive workers receive higher earnings than do time workers in comparable jobs, although the size of differential is not consistent from industry to industry. The earnings advantage of incentive workers ranged from less than 5 per cent to at least 40 per cent in the individual manufacturing industries studied in 1945–46; in many of the industries the difference was between 15 and 25 per cent.

Among the four major manufacturing groups . . . the largest differential appeared in the apparel industries where incentive workers earned from a fifth to two-fifths more than time workers. In the metal working industries, incentive workers most commonly received from a fourth to a fifth more than time workers, whereas in the textile industries the differentials were typically between a sixth and a tenth. The chemical industries, in which incentive pay is relatively unimportant, showed no consistent pattern of differences between time and incentive earnings, although in several of these industries the

[3] United States Department of Labor, Bureau of Labor Statistics, *Effect of Incentive Payments on Hourly Earnings,* Bulletin No. 742 (Washington, U.S. Government Printing Office, 1943), p. 1.

difference was small. Among the nonmanufacturing industries in which incentive pay was most important—automobile repair shops and clothing and department stores—the differential amounted to about a third.[4]

Studies of changes in the level of earnings associated with changing from time wages to wage incentives indicate results similar to the above.

In 1944, the Management Consultant Division of the U.S. War Production Board investigated eighty-six wage incentive installations in the Chicago area. It found that, on the average, workers' earnings increased by 19 percent.[5]

A study made in 1948 showed that earnings of average production employees on incentive, expressed as a percent of straight-time base pay, ranged from 102 percent to 155 percent. The average was 124.4 percent.[6]

No statistical breakdown as to the average bonus earnings was attempted for the plants investigated in the course of this study, but the information gained through available records and interviews corresponds closely with the findings quoted above.[7] For example, in Case No. 23 the

[4] Joseph M. Sherman, "Incentive Pay in American Industry, 1945–1946," *Monthly Labor Review*, LXV (November, 1947), 535–38. The U.S. Department of Labor, Bureau of Labor Statistics, has made a series of studies of industry wage structures. In nearly every case, incentive earnings exceed time earnings for workers in the same occupation. For example, see *Wage Structure: Radios, 1947*, Series 2, No. 2 (Washington, February, 1948). See also National Industrial Conference Board, Inc., *Wage Incentive Practices*, No. 68 in *Studies in Personnel Policy* (New York, 1945); *American Machinist* (January 3, 1946), pp. 97–108; *Management Review*, XXXVII (October, 1948).

[5] United States War Production Board, Addresses and Papers on Wage Incentive Plans and Labor Management Relationships (Mimeographed, October, 1944), IV, 4.

[6] *Management Review*, XXXVIII (January, 1949). Similar results are indicated by the survey made by the Dartnell Corporation, *Experience of 117 Companies with Wage Incentive Plans* (Chicago, 1948), pp. 5–7.

[7] As used in this study, "bonus" refers to earnings in excess of guaranteed hourly rates of pay. For example, if a worker who is guaranteed $1.00 an hour averages $1.50 under the wage incentive system, the extra 50 cents is his bonus. Percentage bonus earned is determined by dividing the bonus by the guaranteed hourly rate of pay.

approximate average bonus was 26 percent; in Case 17, it was 33 percent; in Case 7, it was 30 percent; in Cases 2 and 8, it was 40 percent; and in Cases 1, 9, 15, and 26 it ranged from 40 percent to 50 percent. It should be noted, however, that these percentages are not constant. From time to time they fluctuate quite widely. Furthermore, within a given plant the range of bonus earnings is significant. In most of the cases studied, the incentive bonuses on different jobs within a plant varied from zero to 150 percent.

Operating Problems Associated with the Use of Wage Incentives

The actual operation of wage incentive systems involves numerous problems.[8] The nature of these problems changes little from case to case. In fact, analysis of the field studies of this investigation shows that the differences between the problems encountered in the various cases are essentially differences of degree rather than kind.

In the discussion that follows these common wage incentive problems are described under two classifications: problems involved in setting standards of output, and problems concerned with the maintenance of an acceptable wage structure.[9]

[8] The problems associated with the use of wage incentives have been mentioned by many writers. See David F. Schloss, *Methods of Industrial Remuneration* (3d ed.; Oxford, England, Williams and Norgate, 1898), pp. 60–86; W. D. Stearns, "Wage Payment Systems in Machine Shops," *Machinery*, XXV (August, 1919), 1115–16; Charles B. Going, *Principles of Industrial Engineering* (New York, McGraw-Hill Book Co., Inc., 1911), pp. 120–25; W. D. Forbes, "Why Piece-Work Is Not Satisfactory," *American Machinist*, LII (March 18, 1920), 612; Harrington Emerson, "My Objections to the Piece-Rate Method of Wage Payment," *Industrial Management*, LVII (June, 1919), 470–72; National Industrial Conference Board, Inc., *Some Problems in Wage Incentive Administration*, and *Wage Incentive Practices*, No. 19 and No. 68 in *Studies in Personnel Policy* (New York, 1940 and 1945); *Experience of 123 Companies with Wage Incentive Plans, Section I* (Chicago, Dartnell Corporation, 1944).

[9] It should be pointed out that these classifications are not totally independent of one another. Maintaining an acceptable wage structure is

SETTING STANDARDS OF OUTPUT

One of the distinctive features of all wage incentives is the fact that an explicit standard of output is determined for each job or task. The study of individual cases reveals that in all local plant situations this process involves a fundamental struggle by workers to obtain loose standards of output.[10] The workers recognize that their self-interest is served by maintaining liberal standards and by producing at a rate in excess of the standard.

Workers employ a number of techniques to obtain loose standards. One of the most dramatic is the deception of management representatives as to the nature of jobs and the general conditions affecting production. Workers' ingenuity in deceiving time study men suggests that numerous loose standards are used in industry. Certainly the evidence uncovered in this investigation supports Henry Dennison's statement that ". . . no time study man living is clever enough to best a moderately clever mechanic and discover the true time." [11]

Case No. 6. An illustration of the imagination and inventive faculty of workers was revealed in an interview with a skilled machine operator. This man operated a grinding machine used in the manufacture of roller bearings. He explained that he "put one over on the time study department" by machining his own sample bearing. The sample is the bearing sent down by the engineering department for checking the accuracy of gauges. By manufacturing a sample of smaller dimensions, the worker was able to get increased time for the performance of the operation. All of the scrap manufactured during the period in which the time study was being taken was either smuggled out of the plant or hidden between the walls of the factory.

---

in part a function of setting standards of output. They are, however, sufficiently distinct to be an aid to the organization of the materials.

10 A loose or liberal standard is one the worker can meet without undue effort; a tight standard is one the worker finds difficult to attain.

11 Henry Dennison, "What Can Employers Do about It?" in Stanley Mathewson, *Restriction of Output among Unorganized Workers* (New York, Viking Press, 1931), p. 188.

The same worker reported other deceptions, such as using grinding wheels of small outside diameter and bleeding the hydraulic system on automatic machines.[12]

Case No. 4. A similar example of worker cleverness in outsmarting time study men showed up in a basic steel plant. A former operator on the skin mill recalled how he had succeeded in obtaining a standard of 120 coils per hour for a job on which the workers could easily produce 300 coils per hour. He did this by distorting the tension on the steel. When the time study men requested that the mill be speeded up, the uneven tension on the steel would cause a breakdown.

Most of the time study men interviewed recognized the fact that workers were constantly attempting to obtain loose standards.

Case No. 1. The time study men in an asbestos textile plant reported a variety of attempts by workers to influence standard setting. These included oiling belts on machines to decrease friction and thus to reduce actual machine speeds; saving up defective materials to be used during time studies; using slow drive gears; and surreptitiously cutting yarn to increase down time.

Case No. 7. The supervisor of time study in a plant manufacturing hospital supplies and industrial tapes pointed out that because workers attempt to deceive time study men by introducing false motions and avoidable delays his men frequently rate work methods. That is, they arbitrarily reduce the time allowed for a job in order to discount superfluous motions.

Case No. 4. One of the time study men in a basic steel plant stated: "Whenever I take a time study I am on my guard. I always expect the workers to try to put something over. For example, on the Number 3 slitter, the one that cuts heavy

---

[12] Throughout this report the material gathered in the course of the field study will be presented in this manner. In accordance with the guarantee of anonymity given to the cooperating companies, their names will not be revealed; however, each case situation is assigned a number so that the reader may recognize illustrations descriptive of a single plant.

cartridge steel, the workers stalled so much that I refused to set a rate. On the Number 3 bloomer pit the crane operators introduced all sorts of delays. The most noticeable one was the taking of six to seven minutes to cool their tongs. Normally they take one half minute for this operation. In my study of the Hallden Shear the operator induced long breakdowns by failing to shut down as soon as the material began to cobble." [13]

The slowdown is a second technique used by workers in attempting to obtain loose standards. It involves concerted action by workers to hold production at a level considerably below their potential output. As such, it is both an attempt to deceive time study men and a collective action to coerce management into liberalizing rates.

The relationship between the slowdown and the deception of rate setters is revealed by the fact that frequently the mere suggestion that a time study may be taken will slow up an entire operation.[14]

Case No. 3. This phenomenon is illustrated by the fact that not only did the workers slow down every time a new garment was put into production, but in one case, when a style number was changed without a corresponding change in the product, production immediately dropped.

The existence of a slowdown is usually inferred from changes in productivity. Sudden and severe drops in output associated with the installation of new standards provides prima-facie evidence of a slowdown. For example:

Case No. 2. In a steel fabricating plant the workers protested newly established rates by holding their production to 8,582

[13] Although anecdotal material is presented in quotation form, is should be noted that the statements are only approximations of the wording used. Every attempt has been made to report faithfully the materials gathered in field interviews. However, since most of the data was gathered in friendly, informal conversations, verbatim notes were seldom taken.

[14] This type of slowdown is also reported in Mathewson, *Restriction of Output.*

pieces per eight-hour shift. Normal production was 14,550 pieces per eight-hour shift. At a later date, in protesting the same standard, output dropped to 5,581 pieces per eight-hour shift.

Although it is relatively easy to recognize a slowdown, proving its existence is extremely difficult. Generally the workers rationalize their drop in production in a manner that leaves room for doubt as to the real reason for the decline in output.

Case No. 4. The problem of conclusively proving the existence of a slowdown is illustrated by the experience of a basic steel company. It had installed a new pickling line. While incentive rates were being determined, the workers were paid their previous average hourly earnings. The average output during the period was 279 tons per line turn. At this time 15 men operated the line. From September, 1951, until August, 1952, management applied a new standard to the operation. The workers contested the rate, and during this period the average production per line turn dropped to 179 tons. In an attempt to overcome this slowdown, management at one time assigned a supervisor to each of the workers on the line. Despite this, there was no significant change in productivity.

It is mainly through hindsight that the magnitude of a slowdown is indicated.

Case No. 4. In the pickling line dispute cited above, an arbitration finally established the correctness of management's standard. Soon production jumped from 179 tons per line turn with a crew of fifteen men per turn, to 625 tons per line turn with a crew of nine men per turn.

The economic loss that workers will incur to sustain a slowdown varies from situation to situation. Frequently it is of considerable magnitude.

Case No. 4. One of the costly slowdowns noted during this study was observed in a basic steel mill. The tin plate bundlers were put on a wage incentive plan in the latter part of 1950. At that time the workers were averaging 16 to 17 bundles per day. Time studies revealed that a more realistic output was 66 bundles per day. From the date of the installation of the incentive plan until the time of these observations (March, 1953) the production was pegged at 16 to 17 bundles per day. Because of this the workers have been averaging around $1.615 per hour, rather than the $2.88 they can earn by producing 66 bundles per day.

Another device used by workers to coerce management into setting loose rates is the strike. Most frequently the "quickie" walkout is used. It generally involves a sudden shutdown of a department or section in an effort to force management to make concessions on standards. For example:

Case No. 1. The workers in the Twisting Department were not satisfied with management's disposition of their complaint over a standard. In protest they shut down their machines and marched into their foreman's office. They refused to return to their work until given a guarantee that a more liberal standard would be applied.

Occasionally these wildcat strikes start with a few workers or a department and spread to become general walkouts.

Case No. 4. In a basic steel plant a dispute over the standards on a new pickling line (see above) resulted in a sitdown strike. In four days this spread to a strike of the entire mill. Fourteen thousand workers were involved. The strike resulted in the loss of 366,512 man hours of work, 65,700 tons of basic pig iron production, and 72,800 tons of ingots.

The total cost of these slowdowns and strikes can only be vaguely inferred. The general evidence revealed by this investigation indicates that their costs can be, and frequently are, substantial.

Case No. 2. A steel fabricating plant kept a ten-month record of the approximate loss of production due to work stoppages and slowdowns. It is estimated that, for the period covered, work stoppages resulted in a loss of 26,530 production line man hours and slowdowns cost 1,364 man hours. The following excerpts illustrate the data included in this analysis.

On December 14, 1944, the workers on the oil line in the Pail Assembly Department shut down for thirty-three minutes to protest their piece rate. This caused a loss of production of six man hours.

On August 10, 1945, the pail assembly line shut down for one hour and six minutes to protest a new rate.

On August 13, 1945, the pail assembly line slowed down for eight hours to pressure management into loosening a new rate. During this period production dropped from 14,500 pieces per eight hours to 8,582 pieces.

On August 22, 1945 the pail assembly line was shut down for two hours and sixteen minutes to protest a new rate. This involved a loss of 10.1 man hours.

In the Barrel Department there were a number of slowdowns. From December 17, 1946, to December 27, 1946, production was held to 1,200 barrels per shift. It gradually increased to 2,200 barrels per shift by March 12, 1947. The company maintained that satisfactory performance for this barrel line was 2,400 per shift.

MAINTAINING AN ACCEPTABLE WAGE STRUCTURE

In each manufacturing plant there exists a wage structure which, over a period of time, has become generally accepted. Usually it reflects the relative worth of the various jobs in the plant. In addition, it tends to rank jobs according to their places in the plant's social hierarchy. Moreover, it is a commonly held value judgment that a worker's earnings should reflect the recognized or accepted value of his job as well as his ability in performing on that job.

Wage incentives inject a dynamic element into the

plant's wage structure. Earnings may become divorced from the individual's merit and the recognized value of his job, and the resulting wage structure may cease to conform to prevailing concepts of fairness and justice. This type of distortion in wage structures was common to the cases covered by this investigation.[15]

Case No. 1. An illustration of the distortion that may occur in the wage structure under wage incentives is the experience of a plant manufacturing asbestos products. A comparison of the relative ranking of jobs under a job evaluation plan with the earnings under the incentive plans shows considerable disparity. The table below illustrates this fact. It shows that average hourly earnings including bonus varied widely from the wage structure that would conform with the ranking of jobs according to the job evaluation plan. For example, the job carrying the greatest number of job evaluation points (machinist supervisor) actually received less per hour than a semi-skilled job (pipe covering finisher).

Job Title	Job Evaluation Point Score	Average Straight-time Earnings Including Bonus (In cents)
Machinist Supervisor	355	128
Insulation Dept., Subforeman	331	124
Carding Dept., Subforeman	305	128
Electrician, First Class	304	120
Weaving Dept., Subforeman	298	142
Preparing Dept., Subforeman	281	144
Pipe Covering Dept., Subforeman	241	160
Block Builder, Pipe Covering	236	165
Lead Sawyer, Pipe Covering	223	184
Pipe Covering Builder	211	165
Cloth Loom Weaver	186	121
Spinner, First Class	177	132

[15] Similar findings are reported by Reynolds. He states: "In 1947 and 1948 it was not unusual to find production workers in labor grades 8 or 9 who were taking home more money than maintenance men in grades 3 or 4." Lloyd George Reynolds, *The Structure of Labor Markets* (New York, Harper and Bros., 1951), p. 196. See also Frederick H. Harbison and Robert Dubin, *Patterns of Union-Management Relations* (Chicago, Science Research Associates, 1947), pp. 139–40.

Job Title	Job Evaluation Point Score	Average Straight-time Earnings Including Bonus (In cents)
Finisher Card Operator	171	102
Spoolers	165	81
Hook Machine Operator	162	182
Cloth Cutter, Packing Dept.	159	102
Mix Picker Operator, Preparing	155	126
Twisting Machine Operator, Packing Dept.	155	89
Pipe Covering Finisher	155	156
Cop Winder, Weaving Dept.	145	108
Disintegrator Operator	145	126
Sweeper, Carding Dept.	125	97

Case No. 4. In a basic steel mill the distortion in earnings associated with the use of wage incentives was brought out by the fact that workers in the same job class had widely varying average hourly earnings. For example, in Job Class 9 a Feeder on No. 26 Finishing averaged $2.651 per hour, while a Ross Carrier on a Ram Tractor averaged $1.821 per hour. Furthermore, workers on lower job classes were exceeding the earnings of those on higher rank jobs. For example, Feeders on No. 23 and No. 24 Finishing, both in Job Class 7, averaged $2.75 per hour. This exceeded the earnings of the Feeders on the 72-inch Tandem, who are in Job Class 9; the Catcher and Sticker on the 54-inch Tandem, who is in Job Class 12; and the Welder Operator on the Coil Pickler, who is in Job Class 13.

Variations in earnings that occur under wage incentives give rise to many problems. The more common of these are the development of pressures for the rapid establishment of standards on new jobs, the tendency for wage incentives to be expanded to cover jobs that are not reasonably suited to such a method of remuneration, the development of grievances over standards of output, the development of animosity among rank-and-file workers, the establishment of ceilings on output, and the development of fraudulent practices.

The development of pressures for the rapid establish-

ment of standards on new jobs. The creation of a new job immediately poses the question, "What is the correct standard of output?" Since the answer to this question is directly related to the worker's earnings, the existence of nonrated incentive work induces anxieties among workers. One of the consequences of this may be a slowdown.[16]

The pressure to have the new job rated as soon as possible is frequently initiated by management. However, if the workers suffer losses in earnings while working on nonrated work, they, too, may agitate for prompt setting of standards.

Case No. 1. In the initial installation of wage incentives in an asbestos fabricating plant the application of pressure for the rapid rating of jobs was dramatically illustrated. When the system was partially installed all of the production departments clamored for coverage under the wage incentive plan. Furthermore, in an effort to speed up the rate of installation of standards and to encourage the setting of loose rates, the workers on nonrated jobs slowed down. Under these conditions the plant manager sent the following letter to the supervisor of industrial engineering:

"Let's not have time study bog down on any operation that is going to take a great deal of time to set up rates. The important thing is to get the system spread among the different departments as quickly as possible. . . . I think it would be a good thing to get a weekly report from Mr. —— [the time study engineer] as to what progress he is making. Where you see that he has slowed up for any reason, you can take corrective measures."

The tendency for wage incentives to be expanded to cover jobs that are not reasonably suited to such a method of remuneration. Sound wage incentive systems require the

[16] See pp. 27–29, above. In incentive shops production on nonrated incentive jobs is usually 40 to 50 percent of the normal established by time study. This means that when standards are applied, output more than doubles.

standardization of work. Their satisfactory operation requires that the units of output be definable with precision, and that the conditions of work be maintained with substantial uniformity over periods of time. The variations in earnings occurring under wage incentives brings about pressure for management to ignore these requirements. The workers on unstandardized nonincentive work point out that their earnings decrease relative to those of workers on wage incentive jobs, and they attempt to have the traditional earnings differentials restored. Generally this is manifested as a demand for the installation of a wage incentive system to cover the nonstandardized work.

Case No. 8. In a plant manufacturing hospital supplies the maintenance mechanics argued at length that they should be included under a bonus plan. They pointed out that the production workers were averaging approximately 40 percent bonus.

Case No. 2. In a plant manufacturing metal containers the workers in the Steel Storage Department—the department that distributes raw materials in the plant—filed a grievance to have an incentive plan applied to their work. When management delayed its reply, the workers marched en masse into the general manager's office and demanded a favorable answer to their grievance. In response to this pressure, management installed a group incentive plan. In its haste it failed to study job methods and failed to describe job conditions. Hence, future administration of the plan was hindered. At the time of this study the workers in Steel Storage were earning a bonus of close to 200 percent.

Case No. 4. In a basic steel plant the switchmen and conductors in the transportation department requested that their work be put under an incentive system. Between 1951 and 1952 they submitted four grievances requesting this. The company maintained that the establishment of a wage incentive plan for this type of work violated all principles of sound management. To support their position they hired a responsible and

reputable firm of consultants to study the feasibility of establishing wage incentives for this work. The consultants reported that the jobs failed to meet the standards required by
wage incentives. However, a slowdown and a wildcat strike
led the company to install a specially designed wage incentive
plan for switchmen and conductors.

*The development of grievances over standards of out-
put.* Workers judged the correctness of standards of output by making comparisons between the ease of earning
bonus pay on a specific job with the ease of earning it on
other jobs. Variations in the looseness of standards and the
related variations in earnings bring about numerous grievances. The general tenor of these is that "the standard
on my job should be lowered to allow my earnings to be
consistent with my previous earnings or with earnings of
other workers." Implicit in these grievances is the theory
that a correct standard is one which provides a consistent
bonus.

Case No. 1. This concept is implied by a grievance filed by
the weavers in a plant fabricating asbestos. They asked that
rates be changed so that each weaver could make a fair bonus
no matter what loom was assigned to him.

The theory is implied in a slightly different form in a
grievance submitted by a worker transferred to a new job. His
grievance read: "I worked for months on the press cutting
machine without making a bonus. On the other job he [the
foreman] took me off of I was making a bonus of three to four
dollars a week."

The concept was applied on a plant-wide basis in a grievance
submitted by the workers of the Insulation Department. They
stated:

"We have tried to get on an equal bonus basis with the
other departments, but the way jobs are rated and the way
changes are made from one job to another we can't make it. We
are willing to produce, but we want to see results on our part
so we can get our weekly wages in keeping with the rest of the

shop. As to the rates on most of the jobs in our department, hardly any is within reason. We aren't able to make money in keeping with the other departments."

Case No. 7. Another aspect of this criterion for judging standards was applied in a grievance contesting the rate established after a method change had been made. The workers in the Ligature Department had been averaging $1.75 per hour on a packaging operation. Management improved the method used for packaging and set a new standard that was more in line with those on other jobs in the plant. Under the new standard the workers averaged $1.14 per hour. The workers submitted a grievance arguing that their rate had been cut. Their argument implied that the new rate should be set to allow the same amount of earnings as did the old one.

Although the workers argue for consistency in earnings, the actual application of this criterion is extremely difficult. Consistency by itself is an ambiguous concept. If it is to be a useful measure of the accuracy of rates, the objects being compared have to be precisely defined. Workers, however, often make only those comparisons that substantiate their arguments. They may compare earnings under a given standard with their previous high in earnings, with the high of other workers, or with any other figures that seem to justify loose rates.

The failure to establish a uniform basis of comparison creates confusion. Furthermore, even if uniform comparisons were made, it is doubtful that a high degree of consistency could ever be attained. The reason for this was succinctly stated by one plant manager when he said: "The Good Lord made everything different." Practically every aspect of every job is subject to some variation. Raw materials, machines, and workers vary from hour to hour and day to day.

Furthermore, it is unlikely that a practical measure for precisely correlating effort and output on all jobs can ever be devised. Human skills tend to be specific rather than general. Success in one kind of job does not necessarily correlate with success in other jobs.[17] Consequently, it is difficult for an individual to compare standards on different jobs in terms of required effort. A worker transferred from one job to another may experience an inverse relation between his effort and output on that job as compared with his previous job.

When variations in job conditions are significant, another type of grievance arises. This involves petitioning supervisors for special allowances to compensate for unusual conditions. In such cases the workers usually argue: "We should not be penalized for conditions beyond our control."

Case No. 2. An example of this occurred in a plant manufacturing metal containers. The company changed the raw materials used in manufacturing steel barrels. It began using cold roll steel instead of hot roll. This change brought a grievance from the workers requesting a special downtime allowance when cold roll was being run. When management refused to grant this request, the workers on the barrel line initiated a sit-down strike.

The development of animosity among rank-and-file workers. A contributing factor to friction in the plant is the fact that the structure of earnings under a wage incentive system often violates the workers' concept of justice and fairness. For example, the old-timer who finds that newer men earn more than he is apt to be resentful. The existence of this feeling was indicated by one long-service employee in Case No. 9. He asked the interviewer: "How would you feel if you found that kids who have been around only a few months earn ten to fifteen dollars a week more than you do?"

[17] F. A. C. Perrin, "An Experimental Study of Motor Ability," *Journal of Experimental Psychology*, IV (1927), 24–56.

The resentment against the "unfair" earnings structure may take subtle forms. It may be expressed in terms of general unrest and grumbling about the plant, working conditions, supervision, etc. This type of expression is so elusive that it is difficult to trace the role of wage incentives in its development. Frequently, however, the resentment that is fostered by the wage incentive system is apparent in the relations between workers employed on interrelated work. For example, it was noticed that when the work of one department was dependent upon the work of another department, any failure on the part of the controlling department could lead to interdepartment squabbles.

Case No. 1. This type of discord was noticed in the textile operations of a plant fabricating asbestos. The operations in the yarn division were all interrelated. If earnings in a given department dropped off, the tendency was to put the blame on the workmanship in the preceding department. Over the six-year period during which this case was observed, open arguments occurred between preparing and carding departments, between the spinning and the twisting departments, and between the twisting and the weaving departments.

Discord also tends to develop between wage incentive workers and time wage workers. This arises from the fact that the bonus earnings of incentive workers upset the traditional differential existing between their earnings and those of time wage workers. Consequently, time wage workers argue that they also should be paid an incentive bonus. To pressure management into such action, the time workers seek the support of their fellow workers. If active backing is not obtained, discord between time workers and incentive workers may develop.

Case No. 10. The threat of such discord was observed at a meeting of the union officers of a valve manufacturer. In this plant approximately 80 percent of the workers were employed under a standard hours wage incentive plan. These workers were averaging bonuses of 40 to 50 percent.

A steward representing the time workers gave a forceful argument for union solidarity in forcing management to pay bonuses to time workers. When he noticed that most of those present were cold to his suggestion, he stated: "You had better back us in getting a bonus or we'll see to it that you won't be able to earn one either."

Occasionally friction among workers develops when the plant as a whole is forced into a costly slowdown or strike to support the demands of a special wage incentive group.

Case No. 4. An example of this occurred in a basic steel mill. The workers on a new pickling line embarrassed their union and antagonized their fellow workers by producing at a level which proved that a costly strike of the entire plant had been unwarranted. One of the workers expressed his resentment in the following manner: "Those ——! We went on strike thinking that management was trying to force a tight rate down their throat. Now we know that it was just a bunch of greedy guys trying to clean up. Look what they're earning now!"

A persistent cause of friction in wage incentive departments is the distribution of work. The existence of loose and tight rates means that some jobs can be completed more speedily and easily than others.

Case No. 5. The tendency for workers to pick only soft jobs was noticed in a sewing department of a plant manufacturing women's apparel. To improve material handling, an overhead conveyor had been installed. This conveyor transported work-in-process around the department. The individual operators obtained their work by selecting a batch from the conveyor. Toward the end of the week only the difficult jobs were left on the conveyor. A check study showed that the most difficult jobs rode the conveyor for weeks.

Case No. 7. The type of problem engendered by inconsistencies in standards was stated by one of the foremen in a plant manufacturing hospital supplies and industrial tapes. He stated: "I can't live with an out-of-line rate. No matter what I do the girls accuse me of playing favorites. They take it out on me and the so-called favorites."

A common cause for animosity among rank-and-file workers is the "rate-buster" [18] (the worker who pushes his output to a level considerably above the norm for his peers). The exact techniques used by fellow workers in dealing with rate-busters varies from situation to situation. It appears to be dependent upon the worker's standing in his work group, his recognized skill and ability, and the fear of rate cuts. For example, in Case No. 22 one old-timer was simply approached by the union steward and given a pep talk on the need for group solidarity. In Case No. 23 a rate-buster was subjected to all kinds of verbal insults. In Case No. 1 a rate-buster had his work sabotaged and was completely ostracized by the work group.

In summary, if wage incentives are effective, they stimulate aggressiveness and a spirit of rivalry, which increases the probability of friction and ill-feelings among rank-and-file workers.[19]

The establishment of ceilings on output. One of the per-

[18] For an interesting descriptive report of the disciplining of rate-busters and of their relationship to the work group see: Orvis Collins, Melville Dalton, and Donald Roy, "Restriction of Output and Social Cleavage in Industry," *Applied Anthropology,* V, No. 3 (Summer, 1946), pp. 1–14; Melville Dalton, "The Industrial Rate-Buster: A Characterization," *Applied Anthropology* VII, No. 1 (Winter, 1948), 5–18.

[19] This tendency was summarized by one union officer when he replied to the question: "Would you rather work under a time wage system or a wage incentive system?" He stated: "I prefer time wages. Wage incentives cause much ill feeling among workers. Some are never satisfied with making out on a good rate. They soon kill the job. This causes all kinds of greed and jealousy."

This tendency was noted also by Benjamin Selekman, who expressed it as follows: "Intrinsically, piece rates induce anxiety, if not always competitive aggressions, in contrast to the comparative securities of time rates." See "Living with Collective Bargaining," *Harvard Business Review,* XX (1941), 30.

sistent phenomena observed in the field work of this study was the maintaining of ceilings on output. It was noticed that most workers are participants in a concerted effort to keep bonus earnings below a specified amount.

The maintenance of ceilings on output resembles the slowdown in that both are forms of restricting output.[20] However, the two differ in purpose. The slowdown is a device used to pressure management to set loose standards, whereas ceilings on output are maintained to protect workers from rate cuts and other undesirable management practices. In other words, workers use the slowdown as an offensive weapon and ceilings on output as a defensive device.

Management representatives point to consistent bonus earning as the most frequent evidence of ceilings on output.

Case No. 8. The industrial relations manager in a plant manufacturing hospital supplies stated: "In most of our departments we have unofficial ceilings on output. For example, the girls on the machine making adhesive bandages have made fairly consistent earnings for the past three months."

More direct evidence of ceilings on output comes from interviews with union officers and rank-and-file workers. Generally they report specific limits on bonus earnings.

20 Ceilings on output are part of the broader area covered under the general heading of "Restriction of Output." For discussions of this see Mathewson, *Restriction of Output.* Mathewson found that: (a) restriction of output arose primarily from fear of cuts in incentive rates and of unemployment, and (b) restriction was an important problem among unorganized plants. See also: Burleigh Gardner and David Moore, *Human Relations in Industry* (rev. ed.; Chicago, Richard D. Irwin, Inc., 1950), pp. 180–92; F. J. Roethlisberger and W. J. Dickson, *Management and the Worker* (Cambridge, Mass., Harvard University Press, 1939), Chap. XVIII; Collins, Dalton, and Roy, "Restriction of Output," *Applied Anthropology,* V, No. 3 (Summer, 1946), 1–14; Van Dusen Kennedy, *Union Policy and Incentive Wage Methods* (New York, Columbia University Press, 1945), Chap. IV.

Case No. 23. In a plant manufacturing diesel engines a radial drill press operator stated that he was expected to make exactly 26 percent bonus.

Case No. 10. The local union president of a plant manufacturing valves said: "We try to keep the boys in line. We don't want anyone making more than 50 percent bonus."

Case No. 7. The union business agent for a plant manufacturing hospital supplies and industrial tapes revealed that "in this plant the group has set 30 percent as a ceiling on earnings. A few workers exceed this level; but if they get too far out of line they are properly taken care of."

The manner in which ceilings on output are established is complex. Interviews with those closely associated with setting them reveals that ceilings are determined by trial-and-error adjustments to a variety of forces. Furthermore, ceilings are not constant over time, nor are they always uniform from one department to another in a given plant.

Case No. 1. In this plant each department had its own ceiling on bonus earnings. At one time the ceiling in the weave shop was 52 percent, in the insulation department it was 60 percent, and in the pipe covering department it was 150 percent.

These ceilings only applied to work paid at straight-time rates. For overtime (work paid at time and one half) higher ceilings were recognized.

Case No. 10. The workers in this valve manufacturing plant reported that on overtime work they raise the ceiling on bonus from 50 percent to 180 percent. However, they pointed out that this was so only for very short-run jobs.

The determination of the level of ceilings on output is related to the workers' long-run interests. The workers fear that unrestricted production will lead to rate cuts and reduced earnings. They also fear that high rates of output will become the standard for judging all workers, which may result in pressure being applied to the less productive worker, and may establish a basis for tighter standards on future jobs. Finally, the workers fear that unrestricted output will reduce employment. They see ceilings as a means of insuring a relatively equitable distribution of a limited amount of available work.

The maintenance of ceilings on output is a difficult task. Ceilings, in themselves, pose a paradoxical situation in which the worker's self-interest in maximum earnings is in conflict with the over-all interests of his work group. Often considerable animosity develops among workers over the question of maintaining the group standard of acceptable production. In actual practice the rigidity of ceilings on output is, in part, dependent on the ease with which the work group or its representatives may check the output records of individual workers.

Case No. 1. This point was illustrated by the events that occurred in the weave shop of a plant fabricating asbestos products. The workers had been accustomed to placing their daily production reports in a cigar box on the foreman's desk. The reports were then sent to the front office to be sorted by clock number and to have earnings calculated. One of the clerks in the front office suggested that a special rack be placed in the weave shop to allow workers to file their production reports by clock number. The approximate savings to be gained from the use of such a rack was close to two hours per week.

Once the rack was installed, the average bonus earned in the department dropped. An investigation revealed that the special rack had made it possible for the work group to police the bonus earnings of all of the workers. Many of the operators had been surpassing the established ceiling of 52 percent.

Although evidence of ceilings on output was found in every case covered by this investigation, it is impossible to say exactly how much production is lost through this practice. Norms for judging whether or not a worker is producing at reasonable efficiency are difficult to determine.

Without established norms precise measurement is not feasible. Thus, evidence that workers are maintaining ceilings on output is not, in itself, conclusive proof of worker inefficiency. Many workers may be putting forth their maximum effort to attain the pegged level of production. Consequently, it may be that only the exceptionally fast workers are actually engaging in restrictive practices.

Despite these difficulties in measuring the cost of ceilings on output, the evidence gathered in the course of this study indicates that, at times, significant losses are incurred. The following episodes may be considered as clues to the loss of production resulting from pegged output.

Case No. 3. In a woman's apparel plant it was discovered that many of the workers were leaving the plant early. A study of the practice revealed that at one time one third of the machine operators were working short hours. Many of them came in at 10:00 A.M. and went home at 3:00 P.M.

Case No. 10. At a union meeting of employees of a plant manufacturing valves the workers were debating the best argument they could present to management to justify extending the incentive system to the indirect workers. One of the workers suggested that they emphasize that an incentive for indirect workers would bring about greater cooperation between direct and indirect workers, and, hence, would increase production. This suggestion was laughed down. It was pointed out that present incentive workers would not produce more even if the indirect workers were on an incentive. Most of the men were already making their 50 percent bonus and were having difficulty covering up their idle time. A check of nine incentive workers in the meeting revealed that for the previous work day each had stalled from one and one-half to three hours.

Case No. 9. In a farm equipment manufacturing plant one of the union shop committeemen implied that many workers were idle several hours a day. He stated that his greatest problem was to get men to stay on their jobs after they had made out for the day. "Making out" was defined as earning a 50 percent bonus.

Further evidence of the cost of pegged production is seen in the worker practice of "banking" output. This practice involves the worker or work group's building up a kitty of processed parts or work tickets which may be turned in if and when needed.[21]

Case No. 3. In this plant the girls maintained ceilings on earnings by banking their production tickets. They would not report production above the established ceiling. The excess would be saved and turned in when it would not indicate excessive earnings. One of the women in this plant was promoted to a supervisory position. She automatically went off the incentive plan and consequently could not get credit for her kitty of $80 worth of tickets.

Case No. 23. One of the workers in a diesel engine plant frequently turned in tickets on engines after they had been installed in South America.

Case No. 11. A railroad car manufacturing company went off of piece rate. One worker reported that he was caught with a kitty of $800 worth of parts. Two years after abandoning the incentive system the management of this plant was still running across caches of processed parts hidden on the premises.

The development of fraudulent practices. The use of wage incentives provides workers and lower level supervision with an opportunity to use sharp practices to further their own special interests. Several such practices have been described above. Other activities of this kind center around maintaining a constant level of earnings and/or increasing earnings without related increases in output.

Case No. 26. The falsification of production records to keep earnings from becoming exceptional was noted in a paint manufacturing plant. The industrial engineering department noticed discrepancies between the reported production and material

[21] For examples of the "kitty system" and a discussion of ceilings on output see Don Roy, *How, Why and How Much Do Workers Restrict Output?* (reproduced by the Committee of Human Relations in Industry, University of Chicago, Publication No. 11, July, 1949), p. 14; Roethlisberger and Dickson, *Management and the Worker*, Chap. XVIII.

transferred by the receiving and stores departments. An investigation of the situation revealed that the foreman screened all work tickets. He reported only that level of production which was consistent with the established ceiling on earnings. Any excess production was held in reserve. It was turned in only if current output failed to provide ceiling earnings.

The most frequently encountered falsification of records is associated with the allocation of the workers' time. The usual practice is for workers to balance out earnings on various jobs so that loose rates do not show in the accounting records.

Case No. 23. This is illustrated by a statement of one of the maintenance department workers in a plant manufacturing diesel engines. He pointed out that "the incentive plan for the maintenance department involves a rapid turnover of jobs and the setting of many new rates. Since business declined, the company has been setting tighter rates. During the day the men usually handle several jobs. They push production on the loose jobs and charge some of their time on tightly rated jobs against the loose jobs." In this manner they maintain a fairly high rate of earnings, even though management is setting rates that are more difficult to meet.

Occasionally the workers claim downtime allowances in order to attain a desired level of bonus earnings.

Case No. 2. An illustration of the practice of padding downtime allowances to increase earnings occurred in the barrel department of this plant. In this department the management agreed that downtime for the barrel line would be calculated on the operation of the double seamer, the fastest machine on the line. The workers' technique for increasing earnings was to check out on the double seamer and to keep the rest of the line operating. Then, when a sufficient supply of barrel shells had accumulated to keep the double seamer going at full speed, the workers would check in on it. The chief industrial engineer described the situation as follows: "In 1942 the Company agreed

to let the workers check out for downtime. The double seamer
was the spot where they checked out. When the double seamer
was down the entire line got credit for downtime. The capacity
of the double seamer was 360 barrels per hour. The workers
juggled the distribution of their work time so that the double
seamer would be shown to run at capacity. At one time the
workers claimed to be running the double seamer at 370 barrels per hour. Management called them on this. It pointed out
that they had taken excessive downtime and proved this by
showing that the maximum capacity of the double seamer
was 360 barrels per hour. From that time on we had an average
rate of output of 360 shells per hour, and we had forty to
sixty checkouts per day. The workers continued to claim downtime until the chutes filled up. Then they checked in and ran
at capacity."

Another type of falsification of records revealed by the
field investigation of this study is the misrepresentation
of reported production.

Case No. 7. In this case it was reported that the accounting
department had discovered a discrepancy between the sale of
scrap paper and the production reported on labor tickets. The
quarterly records showed: 1st quarter, 32,575 pounds reported
baled and 47,108 pounds sold; 2d quarter, 35,459 pounds reported baled and 49,838 pounds sold; 3d quarter, 42,017 pounds
reported baled and 57,942 pounds sold. Investigation of this
situation revealed that, because of low bonus earnings on baling
of corrugated paper, the worker had charged his time for that
work to time wage work.

A practice closely related to cheating but more subtle is
sacrificing of quality for quantity. The tendency for wage
incentive workers to increase the quantity of their output
while reducing its quality has been noted by many writers.
The observations made in the course of this investigation
tend to substantiate these earlier reports. It was noted
that, in situations in which management had not estab-

lished close controls, wage incentive workers tended to sacrifice quality of product, care of equipment, and economy in the use of raw materials for quantity of output.

Case No. 23. In a plant manufacturing diesel engines a radial drill press operator stated that he generally ran his machine with speeds and feeds in excess of those specified. He recognized that this increased the cost of cutting tools, but justified his actions on the grounds that it gave him greater freedom in setting his own work pace.

Case No. 15. In a plant fabricating pipe covering the workers discovered that they could reduce the number of rejected sections if they increased the density of the product. Since the workers were not penalized for overweight sections, they were not concerned about the increase in material costs and drying time. One foreman summarized the situation by saying: "The incentive system puts these guys into business for themselves, and it's to hell with the company. With these sections running overweight it's just like putting a dollar bill in every carton."

MANAGEMENT ACTIVITIES ASSOCIATED WITH THE ADMINISTRATION OF WAGE INCENTIVES

Management's activities with respect to wage incentives are directed at avoiding or solving the problems discussed above. For purpose of discussion these may be grouped as: (1) explaining the wage incentive system to employees, (2) setting and maintaining sound standards, (3) installing the standard, (4) avoiding or correcting inequities in the wage structure, and (5) preventing fraudulent practices.

EXPLAINING THE WAGE INCENTIVE SYSTEM TO EMPLOYEES

The first step in installing a wage incentive plan is explaining it to the workers. A common practice reported in this investigation is for management to explain, in a fairly complete manner, the details of its wage incentive plan. It should be noted, however, that this explanation is generally limited to the initial installation of the incentive plan. None of the plants studied had a sustained program for explaining wage incentives to rank-and-file workers.

A few of the companies reported that they explained their wage incentive plans in the employee's handbook. However, requests for the handbook met the answer: "At the present time, our handbook is out of print." Interviews revealed that the statements in the employee's handbook are general. The following example illustrates their usual form.

The Management of Plomb Tool Company believes that payment for production work should be based upon several fundamental principles, as follows:

1. It is the policy of the Company to guarantee hourly base rates regardless of how low an employee's production may temporarily fall.

2. Consistent failure to produce up to standard is considered evidence of incapability and, therefore, cause for dismissal.

3. The Company shall have sole right to determine what method and equipment shall be used in the performance of an operation.

4. A time standard is set on one method only. When a standard is properly established so long as the standard procedure is followed, the standard is guaranteed against changes regardless of how much an employee earns.

5. Payment of operators shall be in proportion to production. After the standard has been met, a bonus for extra performance is given. A separate fund amounting to one-third of the bonus given is set aside for division among indirect operators for their indirect contribution to the direct operator's production.

6. When the method used on an operation deviates from the standard practice in any way, regardless of who makes the change, a new standard must be set by accepted time study methods.

7. Suggestions made by employees for changes in method will be paid in accordance with the established suggestion award procedure.

8. When a standard is improperly set in the opinion of either employees or the management and when either desires to adjust the standard in the interest of maintaining equitable differentials in and proper cost of production, the management will attempt to reach an agreement with employees. If an agreement cannot be amicably reached by employees and management, then the machinery for handling grievances will be employed.[22]

Frequently information such as the above is included in the labor-management agreement.

Case No. 22. One of the most detailed agreements regarding wage incentives was made between a plant manufacturing steel castings and the United Steelworkers of America. The agreement provided, in part:
"Standard hour incentive rates shall be established by the Company so that the average incentive employee shall be able to earn at least twenty-five per cent above his classified rate of pay. . . . A new or changed incentive standard shall not be subject to any grievances contending that the standard is incorrect until the job has been in production for eighty working hours. During the next eighty working hours while the job is in production, the Union shall have the right to file a grievance. . . . If no grievance is filed, the standard becomes permanent at the end of one hundred and sixty working hours and may not be changed except as provided in Section 4. . . . If a grievance is filed, the standard resulting from the settlement of the grievance becomes permanent. In the event an adjustment is made in a standard as a result of a grievance, the adjustment shall be made retroactive to the installation of the standard. . . . Once a standard becomes permanent, there shall be no change in the standard unless there is a measurable change in the tooling, methods, materials or operations, and

22 National Industrial Conference Board, Inc., *Wage Incentive Practices,* No. 68 in *Studies in Personnel Policy,* pp. 24–25.

in that event, the change in the standard shall only be to the extent of such change in the tooling, methods, materials or operations. . . . All incentive earnings shall be guaranteed daily. . . . The classified rates for all jobs shall be guaranteed at all times. . . . An incentive worker or group incentive crew shall receive credit only for work which is of acceptable quality. . . . All downtime, beyond the control of the operator, shall be paid for at the classified rate of pay. . . . No employee shall be penalized for refusal to work at incentive pace.

"In the event of a dispute as to the correctness of a standard, an earnest effort shall be made to dispose of the dispute in the following manner: (a) The Grievance Committeeman in the department where the dispute arose, together with the employee involved and the Foreman and the Company Time Study Man shall attempt to settle the dispute. (b) In the event the dispute cannot be settled in Step (a) above, the matter shall then be processed under the grievance procedure. . . . It is specifically understood that a representative of the Union shall be afforded the right at any reasonable time to make a check study of any standard in dispute.

"A copy of all methods and time studies shall be given to the Union prior to the installation of any standard. No standard will be installed unless this provision is fulfilled.

"Before a time study shall be made, the employees shall be notified that the study is to be made, and the method will be thoroughly explained.

"When a regular incentive operator or a regular group incentive crew is required to suspend incentive work for the purpose of making samples, the worker or workers involved shall be paid twenty per cent above their regular base rate or rates for the time spent on such work.

". . . Short order work shall be assigned whenever practical to the junior worker or workers in the applicable classification. For the purposes of the Section, short order work is defined as work performed in connection with the manufacturer of castings where the quantities are insufficient, from an engineering standpoint, to permit establishment of incentive standards."

Case No. 7. In contrast with the above a plant manufacturing

hospital supplies and industrial tapes limited its agreement
regarding wage incentives to: "An employee shall be paid
for waiting time at his or her time work rate. Waiting time
does not include a period of one-tenth of an hour or less for
piece workers. . . . Any alleged unfair piecework rate shall
be handled as a grievance. In the event an adjustment is
found to be justified, such adjustment shall be retroactive
to the time the grievance was submitted in writing to the Works
Manager. . . . A piecework employee shall be given the minimum guarantee rate for the classification of work in which
the piecework job is classified in the event he or she fails
to earn as much as the minimum on piecework."

Most of the agreements fall somewhere between these
two extremes. They define the union's role in setting up
or protesting standards and provide the workers with guarantees against rate cutting.[23]

[23] In contrast with the findings of this investigation, a more compre-
hensive study by the Bureau of National Affairs reveals that:
"Union participation in rate setting is basically of three types: (1) The
union negotiates all rates and its agreement is necessary before any rate
may be made effective. (2) The union is consulted in advance but the
company retains the right to institute the rate even without approval,
subject to subsequent union grievance action. (3) The company has full
control over determination of rates, subject only to grievance action by
the union after the rate is put into operation.
"The first practice, joint determination, is prevalent in the apparel industries. Elsewhere, less than 2 percent of incentive provisions call for such
procedure. Most often, this full and equal union participation accompanies
simple piece rate systems. Arbitration is normally used to resolve disagree-
ments.
"Prior discussion with the union, before installation of the rate, is in-
creasingly common. Almost a quarter of incentive clauses embody this
requirement. A sizable portion of them, however, are confined to textile
and steel industry agreements. Under this procedure, if the union fails to
agree on the rate, it is usually on trial for a specified number of days or
weeks. A grievance may then be filed and, ordinarily, processed through
arbitration if necessary.
"But the most frequent means of rate setting is still unilateral determination by the company, subject to union complaint. Although only
a quarter of incentive provisions spell this out as their procedure, it is
apparent that this is ordinarily the means used where the contract does
not refer to union participation. Here, too, however, the union may under
most contracts dispute the rate up to arbitration for final adjustment."

Usually they include statements that rates will be guaranteed as long as job content or method of operation are unchanged. In addition, they may contain clauses guaranteeing minimum earnings to incentive workers, regulating the selection of workers to be timed, restricting the use of temporary incentive rates, stating time study procedures, and protecting workers against secret time studies.[24]

Available evidence indicates that in actuality wage incentives are explained to workers by their supervisors. To facilitate this, most companies develop a formal or informal program for training supervisors in wage incentive techniques. The training of supervisors is frequently carried on in formal classes covering motion and time study as well as wage incentive policies. Such classes may be taught by outside consultants or by the plant industrial engineer.

Formal class sessions usually are supplemented with personal consultations between supervisors and the plant's industrial engineer.

Case No. 2. The chief industrial engineer in a plant manufacturing metal containers explained that "our foremen have an excellent working knowledge of the wage incentive system. I have personally spent four to five hours in private conferences with each supervisor."

Bureau of National Affairs, Inc., *Basic Patterns in Collective Bargaining Contracts* (Washington, 1949), pp. 15:404–15:405.

For other studies of union contract clauses concerning wage incentives, see United States Department of Labor, Bureau of Labor Statistics Bulletins No. 717, *Incentive Wage Plans and Collective Bargaining,* and No. 686, *Agreement Provisions* (Washington, U.S. Government Printing Office, 1942).

[24] For samples of clauses covering these and related areas, see United States Department of Labor, Bureau of Labor Statistics, *Incentive Wage Provisions* (Preliminary Draft, April, 1947), and *Time Studies and Standards of Production* (Preliminary Draft, June, 1947). These studies contain illustrative clauses selected from the 15,000-odd collective bargaining contracts on file in the Industrial Relations Branch of the United States Department of Labor.

This same company provides its foremen with a detailed manual on wage incentives. The following is taken directly from this foreman's manual. It is quoted in considerable detail to illustrate the formal procedures developed for dealing with common wage incentive problems.

"The wage incentive plan in use in the factory is a type of Manchester plan, that is, a straight piecework system with a daily guarantee. Piecework prices are established by means of time studies, and are guaranteed against any change, except when methods, tools, equipment or layout are altered.

"The primary responsibility for reporting any change in methods, tools or equipment rests with the Foreman. He is assisted in this function of his job by the Timekeeping, Engineering and Time Study departments, but since the Foreman is closer to the jobs being run than the Engineering and Time Study personnel, and generally has greater technical knowledge than the timekeeper, he will be most likely to know of any changes before any one else.

"Experience has shown that the difficulty of making adjustments in incentive rates increases in direct proportion to the length of time that elapses between the change and the rate adjustment.

"When any changes do occur, or when operators request a check study, the Foreman notifies the Time Study Department or his production supervisor that he wants to have a time study made. This is done by filling out a 'Request for a Time Study' form, available in the Time Study Office or in the Production Supervisor's office. On this form he will give the job to be studied, the reason for the request, and the date and time of day the job is to be run. After signing the form he gets it approved by the Factory Superintendent or the Assistant General Production Supervisor and gives it to the Time Study Department. He then notifies the department steward and the people whose job is to be studied that a Time Study Observer has been called to look at the operation. At this time he will inform the people that if a piecework price can be developed from the study, they will have the price applied from the start of the job, otherwise they will be paid average earnings.

"The Time Study Observer makes an elemental breakdown of the job by dividing up the job on the time study form into a series of short, distinct operations that are practical to time. The recorded times are leveled to a normal time by an application of a percentage figure (100 percent being normal), depending on the performance the operator exhibited while the study was being made. The leveled time has allowances added to it for relief, fatigue, and miscellaneous delays and the time is then converted to a piecework price.

"When the study has been developed into a piecework price, the Foreman and a representative of the Time Study Department go over all the factors involved to be sure all necessary elements of the job are included. When the Foreman is satisfied that the time study covers the job, he signs the study. It is then signed by the General Factory Superintendent or his assistant, and issued for application to the Timekeeper of the department.

"Credit for production on the incentive plan, as well as listing all time worked, by correct labor account numbers usually is the responsibility of the Timekeeper, but he must have the cooperation of the Foreman. The Timekeeper depends on the Foreman to instruct the operators in the correct work methods to follow, the proper way to check in and out on a job and to answer any questions regarding the application of the incentive plan. The Timekeeper, in turn, must notify the Foreman of any irregularities in job conditions, such as variations in methods, tools, workplace, layout or the number of people used on the job.

AVERAGE EARNINGS

"The process by which the Payroll Department develops an average earning rate is explained elsewhere in this Policy Manual. It is the purpose of this section to explain the theory and conditions under which payment of average earnings is made.

"Average earnings is a form of Maintenance of Earnings. The thought behind the payment of average earnings is that an employee is entitled to the rate of pay that he regularly earns on piecework, when he is assigned to a job that would normally be classified as a piecework operation but which has had no piecework price established. This does not mean that payment of average earnings is indicated simply because a price has not been established when the employee starts the job. The procedure set up by our labor contract is to make a piecework price retroactive to the start of the job after the price has been developed and approved. Deviation from this contract provision is made for the following reasons:

"1. Because the quantity run is small or other work prevents the time study observer from seeing the job, the run is completed before a study can be made.

"2. Mechanical or process troubles prevent application of a standard method of operation.

"3. More than one method is used to do the operation due to application of methods or improvements during the course of the job.

"4. It is definitely known that the job as it is run at present will have changes in method, tools, equipment, materials or workplace layout within a reasonable length of time.

"Because an average earning rate is always greater than a basic daywork pay rate, we have a right to expect a good day's work from any employee compensated in this way. Too often, we receive a sub-standard performance on such jobs unless the Foreman explained to the people that he will expect a conscientious effort in return for the extra money they receive, and then checked performances on average earnings often enough to demonstrate his interest in the progress of the work.

"Before notifying employees that they will be paid average earnings, the Foreman should first check with the Time Study Department to be sure no piecework price exists, or no price can be developed for the job as it is being run. He then contacts the General Factory Superintendent or his assistant to get approval for payment on this basis. To notify the Payroll Department that the operation is authorized for average earnings, the Foreman will make out a request in triplicate on the inter-office communication form, to the General Factory Superintendent, giving the part number, the quantity if the request is for one run only, and the reason for not using a piecework price. He then has the head of the Time Study and the General Factory Superintendent or their assistant initial the request. One copy goes to the Payroll Department, one to the Factory Superintendent, and one copy is retained by the Foreman for his file. The Authorization remains in effect only as long as the conditions which initiated the request exist, and will apply only to those part numbers listed."

SETTING AND MAINTAINING SOUND STANDARDS

One of management's constant problems in incentive plants is the setting and maintaining of sound standards of output. The usual procedure for working toward this goal is the establishing of a time study specialist to study jobs systematically. The exact position of the time study man in the organization varies from situation to situation. In the cases covered by this investigation the prevailing pattern is for the time study men to be included in a staff department handling industrial engineering responsibilities. The history of this special department usually is traceable to the growth and development of the wage incentive system. Furthermore, there is a noticeable tendency for the time study men to expand their functions to include production scheduling, quality control, cost accounting, and wage administration.

Case No. 3. The time study man originally worked under the plant manager. Later he had his own department. Gradually the duties of that department expanded to include responsibility for methods work, quality control, production scheduling, cost estimating, and sales forecasting.

Case No. 1. Originally the time study man reported to the plant manager. Later he was placed under the direction of the master mechanic. Next he was put in the cost department and finally, a standards department was established. The standards department was primarily responsible for setting rates. However, in time, it took on the staff responsibility for cost accounting, job evaluation, union negotiations, and worker training.

Time study is the common technique used for setting standards. Most of the plants studied relied on stopwatch studies similar to those described by F. W. Taylor.[25] In several plants the results of time studies were assembled to provide standard data.[26] This was most frequent where numerous short-run jobs occurred. For example:

Case No. 3. In a women's apparel plant there were frequent style changes. To cope with the situation, the industrial engineers developed standard data. In this manner they could set standards on new styles as soon as the specifications were known.

The most recently popularized techniques of building time standards from basic motion times were not used in the plants visited in this study. It should be pointed out, however, that many of the industrial engineers had taken courses in the use of systems such as Methods Time Measurement (MTM), Motion Time Analysis (MTA) and Work Factor. The reason for not using these techniques was explained by one industrial engineer. He stated: "I have been trained in the use of synthetic times, but I seldom use them for setting standards. The main reason for this is that the workers are suspicious of rates that aren't based on stopwatch time studies."

INSTALLING THE STANDARD

Once a tentative standard has been set, it remains to have it approved and installed. Furthermore, provision

[25] See p. 81.

[26] Standard data are an extension of the application of conventional time study. This involves the use of elemental time values, determined by time studies, in setting standards on new jobs. Whenever a new job is encountered, it is broken down into elements and the times for these elements are determined from previous studies. This method increases consistency between standards on related jobs and simplifies the process of setting rates.

should be made for handling grievances over the new rate. The procedure for approving new standards varied from plant to plant. In one company the time study man was the only person who approved rates before they became effective. In another company the new rate had to be approved by the proper foreman, the time study man, and the plant manager. In still another several labor relations officers, the accounting department, and the line officials all had to approve a rate before it could be applied.

The method of informing workers of new standards varied. In several plants the workers learned of new standards as jobs were assigned; in others the management sent a copy of the new standard to the union; and in one plant all new standards were posted on the bulletin board.

Case No. 2. An interesting procedure for securing worker acceptance of new standards was observed in a plant manufacturing metal containers. In this plant the responsibility for approving new rates was placed on the foremen. In actual practice the foremen cleared all new rates with the union, so that any objections to the new standard could be discussed on an informal basis. In this manner serious grievances over the acceptability of rates were minimized.

Most of the management representatives interviewed reported that if a grievance over standards did arise, it could seldom be settled by arguing the accuracy of the time study. They justified this either by asserting that the workers "don't understand time study," or by pointing out that, since time study is not a science, there is room for considerable disagreement over the correctness of standards. The general procedure for settling disputes over rates is to have the workers or their representatives make a cursory time study of the work in question. For example:

Case No. 2. The general manager of a plant manufacturing metal containers pointed out that the only way in which he could settle grievances over standards was to watch the work being performed. He stated: "I don't usually let the time study man participate in our check studies. He is a source of friction and a focal point of worker resentment. Instead, I get the union representative and we both watch the job. The foreman is also in on it. He makes certain that the correct method is used. After we watch the job for a while, I ask the union representative to note the rate of output and to compare it with the contested standard.

Case No. 3. The chief industrial engineer of a plant manufacturing women's apparel reported: "We settle grievances over rates by having the girls watch the job in operation. If this doesn't end the dispute, we come up to the conference room and I give them a detailed explanation of the standard. Frequently I use motion pictures of the job to prove my point."

In several of the cases covered by this investigation the local unions had men trained in industrial engineering techniques. Even so, these unions are careful to avoid direct participation in setting rates. Their principal function is to represent workers in processing grievances.

Case No. 22. A plant manufacturing steel castings has two union men designated as time study stewards. These men are trained in time and motion study. Their function is to make check studies of contested rates. On the basis of their studies they advise the grievance committee. The main purpose is to prevent the union from being embarrassed by processing grievances that are obviously unjustified.

When the union and management cannot settle a standards problem, they may submit it to arbitration. However, some of the companies covered by this investigation steadfastly refuse to let any third party settle grievances over standards.

Case No. 2. In a plant manufacturing metal containers the vice-president in charge of production emphasized that he would never go to arbitration on a grievance over incentive standards. He stated that he did not want any outsider settling these cases. To point out the importance placed on this, he recalled how in 1946 one of the principal issues of the 191-day strike was whether or not rate cases would go to arbitration.

Although most management representatives try to discourage it, the use of arbitration to settle wage incentive grievances is an accepted practice. The reason for this was suggested by an international representative of one of the large C.I.O. unions. He frankly admitted that many of the incentive rate cases have political origins. Weak cases are brought up which, for political reasons, cannot be dropped. The only way to dispose of these cases is to carry them to arbitration and let the arbiter act as a scapegoat for the unpopular decision.

Case No. 4. The need to arbitrate standards grievances is illustrated by the problem encountered in installing rates on a new pickling line. Management and the union struggled to determine the new rate. Because of union politics the case could not be dropped. A sustained slowdown and a costly strike failed to settle the issue. As a final effort, both parties agreed to arbitrate the case.

The arbitration of wage incentive disputes usually follows the established grievance procedure. Occasionally, however, a special arbitration procedure for settling wage incentive disputes is written into the labor-management agreement. One such clause reads as follows:

Case No. 19. "Any dispute as to the equity of a job standard or the evaluation of a particular job not settled as provided above shall not be subject to the arbitration procedure provided in Article X, but shall be settled as follows:

"(a) The services of an impartial industrial engineering concern chosen from the list shown below shall be secured. The concern so chosen shall appoint, as a consultant, an engineer experienced and expert in the particular field who shall make an actual study of the disputed job standard or job evaluation. If the dispute involves a job standard, the consultant shall determine whether the standard is equitable. If the dispute involves a question of job evaluation, the consultant shall determine whether there has been a change in job conditions since installation of the previous rate, and if so, whether the new rate is based upon proper application of the Company's established job evaluation plan for job rating.

"(b) If the consultant finds that a job standard is inequitable or that a job has been evaluated improperly, as hereinabove defined, he shall establish a proper standard or re-evaluate the job as the case may be, in all accordance with the general principles of the Company's established plans for setting job standards and for job evaluation.

"(c) Any adjustment agreed upon in Section 5 above or any findings and decisions reached by the consultant shall be final and binding upon both parties for the duration of this Agreement unless further modifications are made in accordance with, and as provided in, this Article."

AVOIDING OR CORRECTING INEQUITIES IN THE WAGE STRUCTURE

Management is confronted with a double problem in maintaining an equitable wage structure. It must attempt to maintain consistent differentials between (a) the earnings of workers on incentive pay and those of workers on time pay, and (b) the earnings of workers on different incentive jobs.

Failure to maintain the first type of differential leads to pressures to extend the wage incentive system to jobs that are not standardized and for which it is difficult to measure output (such as stockroom work and maintenance department work). In this study three general types of solutions to this problem were observed.

One approach used by management to cope with this situation was to give nonincentive workers a bonus based upon the earnings of incentive workers. The use of this procedure has been described by Harbison and Dubin in their case study of the Studebaker plant. They report:

The incentive wage system gave rise to a considerable spread between the pay for hourly and incentive workers. . . . Both the union and the company recognized it as a problem. An answer finally worked out was to put indirect labor on incentive also, with incentive pay tied to the output of the productive workers served.[27]

A second method of dealing with this problem involved increasing the base pay of nonincentive workers and labeling the increase a bonus.

Case No. 15. In a plant manufacturing pipe coverings, the management attempted to correct inequities between maintenance workers and incentive workers by giving the former a flat increase in earnings. This increase, which amounted to 25 percent, was separated from regular hourly pay so as to identify it as a bonus. In actuality, this was not an incentive system. Explicit standards of performance were not set, nor was bonus directly related to output.

The third approach to this problem involves putting time workers on special incentive plans, which are usually based on group rather than individual output.

Case No. 8. To provide the maintenance mechanics with an opportunity to earn bonus, a special group incentive plan was installed. Under it the mechanics earned a bonus calculated on the ratio of maintenance hours to the output of the plant. The output of the plant was calculated in terms of units translated into standard costs as of a given date.

Case No. 1. In a plant manufacturing asbestos products, the management was faced with the problem of correcting a distortion of the wage structure in the insulation department, in which 90 percent of the work was covered by a Halsey 50-50 premium bonus plan. The workers in the department averaged between 40 and 60 percent bonus.

In 1946 the department began to get a number of special orders for tailor-made insulations. Since these specials were for

[27] Harbison and Dubin, *Union-Management Relations*, p. 139.

nonstandardized and nonrepetitive work, the company refused to include them under the incentive system.

The workers assigned to this special work received a flat bonus of 25 percent. Due to the requirements of the job, only the most skilled workers were assigned to the special orders. These were the workers who had been averaging approximately 60 percent bonus. Several grievances were submitted by these employees. They argued that they were being penalized for being skilled in their work, and that if the less skilled men couldn't be assigned to the special work, the company should at least guarantee the men their average earnings.

In response to these grievances, management installed a special group bonus plan. The Rowan formula was used for relating output to bonus. Consequently, the danger of out-of-line earnings was mitigated. The standards used for the special jobs were determined by loose estimates.

A written explanation of the bonus plan was presented to the union and the workers appeared to be reasonably satisfied with the system. They applied themselves to their jobs, designed new fixtures and otherwise increased production so that they averaged 50 percent bonus.

Management techniques for maintaining equitable earnings differentials between incentive jobs included the following.

Granting special allowances to maintain worker earnings. Some managements attempt to avoid extreme drops in workers' bonus earnings by providing that under certain specified conditions the workers will be given their average earnings.

Case No. 3. An example of this occurred in a plant manufacturing women's apparel. The chief industrial engineer pointed out that: "We try to maintain the workers' earnings. We build an allowance of fifteen minutes a day into our standards. In the event that such things as bad materials and machine downtime cause greater delays, we generally pay the girl her average earnings."

Gradually loosening standards. In some companies management attempts to keep bonus earnings fairly consistent by setting new standards at a level in line with average earnings.

Case No. 2. This practice was observed in a plant manufacturing metal containers. The supervisor of industrial engineering reported: "Originally we set standards to allow 20 percent bonus; however, in view of the gradual loosening of standards, we now set them so that a normal worker can earn 40 percent."

Helping to maintain ceilings on output. In several plants management consciously or unconsciously contributes to the maintenance of ceilings on output. In several cases this developed from the practice of supplying the union with details on the bonus earnings of the workers. In other cases it grew out of the activities of the foremen and lower level supervisors.

Rotating work assignments. Frequently lower level supervisors attempt to maintain a reasonable wage structure by allocating work so as to give each worker an equal opportunity to work on loose and tight standards.

Case No. 7. The foreman of an assembly department reported that this was his usual procedure: "The only way I can avoid accusations of favoritism is to rotate the girls so that each gets her share of loose rates."

Introducing methods changes. Another device for maintaining a reasonable structure of earnings is the use of methods changes. In most cases management guarantees standards of output only so long as the method of work is unchanged. Thus, the legitimate means for correcting an out-of-line rate is to change the method.

Case No. 1. An illustration of this was revealed in a report by the supervisor of standards to the executive vice-president of the company. It read:

"Bonus inequities in the plant should be corrected. . . . An analysis of the records shows that four departments have average bonuses that are out of line. . . . The situation in the first department may be partially corrected by improving the layout of machinery (e.g., a conveyor could be used to carry opened stock to the pickers). The installation of such a machine would justify a change in bonus standards. In [the second department] the situation may be corrected by installing an automatic conveyor which will coat, dry and wind six to twelve lengths of tape at one time."

It should be pointed out that methods changes are not limited to use as an excuse for tightening standards. In some cases they were used to loosen standards and thereby to increase earnings.

Case No. 1. In this plant the twisting department workers complained that their bonus potential was low compared to that of workers in other departments. Rather than lower the standard for the work, management speeded up the machines and thus increased the bonus potential of the workers.

PREVENTING FRAUDULENT PRACTICES

A business agent of the Textile Workers of America, C.I.O., stated: "Management is continually thinking of new ways to check production records and to set up a fool-proof system. The workers spent a lot of time figuring out how to beat these systems. Usually the workers find an easy way out."

The results of this investigation support this observation. Management usually attempts to prevent workers from cheating. One method of doing this is to cross-check actual production with that reported on labor tickets.

Case No. 1. An example of this occurred in a plant fabricating asbestos. The standards department compared materials transferred between departments with production reported on labor tickets. When this check was first instigated, it was discovered that, on many jobs with tight rates, labor tickets were never turned in. Instead the workers misrepresented such work in order to get the benefits of looser rates.

Another management technique for maintaining honest records is to hire timekeepers for each department. Usually the timekeepers report directly to a staff officer. Their function is to distribute labor cards and to see that workers have properly recorded their work time and output.

To simplify making production counts, many companies install special counters on their machines. For example, a loom can have a Veeder Root counter mounted on it so that the footage of cloth will be readily determined. Frequently the plants use special mechanical downtime recorders on machines where this factor is important. The inadequacy of devices such as these was indicated by this investigation.

Case No. 2. The company used special charts for recording machine running time. These charts worked on the basis of electrical contacts made when the machine was running. One of the workers revealed that his gang had figured out how to short the recorder and thus show downtime when in actuality the machine was running.

Case No. 15. To record production on looms used for making asbestos blankets, the company installed a meter that registered the number of picks made during the work day. The workers beat this system by removing the pulley driving the meter and then turning up the meter by hand.

Case No. 1. To record machine downtime, the company installed Servis Recorders. The Servis Recorder is a simple device consisting of a clock with a long stylus for a hand. When the machine is in operation, the stylus vibrates and scratches a broad band on the waxed face of the clock. The standards department found that these recorders failed to work. The reason for this became evident when one worker was observed hitting a recorder with a sledge hammer.

An Evaluation of the Impact of Wage
Incentives on Costs

The evidence gathered in this empirical study indicates
both desirable and undesirable results arising from the use
of wage incentives.

On the positive side it is evident that:

1. Wage incentives can contribute to increased worker
output. In a number of instances rank-and-file workers reported that "when the wage incentive plan was put in we
began to help each other and we really increased our output." Furthermore, in certain instances the wage incentive
system forced workers to devise improved work methods.

Case No. 23. This latter point was illustrated in the case
of a plant producing diesel engines. In the testing department
the management set such tight standards that the men couldn't
make a bonus. After numerous grievances the workers were con-
vinced that management would not lower its rates. Once this
conviction was established, the workers cooperated to increase
output. By close cooperation and reassignment of job duties
they figured a better way of doing the job and thus they were
able to earn what they considered an adequate bonus.

2. Wage incentives provide management with a device
for circumventing wage stabilization laws. In this they aid
in attracting and holding workers.

Case No. 26. An example of this use of wage incentives was
cited by the chief industrial engineer in a firm manufacturing
paints. He pointed out that during the World War II emergency the company installed a wage incentive plan in the drum
cleaning department. Loose standards were set to provide a
level of earnings that would be helpful in attracting and holding help.

3. Wage incentives allow management considerable
flexibility in adjusting to changing market conditions. This

point is closely related to point Number 2 above. The reason for separating the two is to emphasize the fact that wage incentives allow downward adjustments in labor costs.

Case No. 10. The downward flexibility of labor costs arising under a wage incentive system is illustrated by the experience of a valve manufacturer. In late 1952 orders began to fall off and price competition became keen. To cut costs the company made the workers absorb in their productive time all downtime. Special delay allowances were discontinued. In addition, minor methods changes were made to provide management with an excuse for tightening standards of output. The workers recognized the need for cutting costs, and consequently they were not militant in resisting these changes.

The tendency for wage incentives to increase the flexibility of labor costs was summed up by a District Representative of the United Steelworkers of America, C.I.O. He pointed out:

At the present time [November, 1953] employers in our plants are tightening up on standards. The recession has forced them to take a strong stand on rate setting, and the union isn't in a position to fight this. It isn't like the war days when companies were willing to let up on rates so as to get around wage stabilization.

4. A fourth benefit attributed to wage incentives is the fact that they force management to do a better job of managing. This opinion was stated by the supervisor of masons in a plant manufacturing steel products. He said:

The real benefit of our incentive plan isn't the increased effort put forth by the workers. It is the fact that as a result of the installation of wage incentives, we set up proper work methods and determined realistic standards of performance. The wage incentive system has caused us to maintain the best working conditions and to do a better job of scheduling production.

The negative aspects of wage incentives have been discussed above under the heading of operating problems. They include tendencies toward deception of time study men, slowdowns, strikes, pressure for rapid rating of incentive jobs, pressure to apply the incentive idea to work that is neither standardized nor measurable in meaningful units, grievances over standards, ceilings on output, fraudulent practices, and friction and animosity among workers.

To these costs of wage incentives should be added:

1. Wage incentives usually require special administrative personnel. In the cases studied in this investigation it was noticed that the use of wage incentives was associated with the hiring of special personnel to handle time study, timekeeping, inspection, and payroll calculations.

Case No. 2. The need for such extra help is illustrated by the complexity of the payroll calculations in a plant manufacturing steel containers. This company had followed the postwar pattern of wage increases. Because of the piecework system it was forced to put the general wage increases into a separate side-rate for each worker. Thus, at the time the plant was studied, each worker had (a) an incentive base rate that was guaranteed for all incentive work; (b) an evaluated base rate that the worker received under special conditions; (c) an average hourly earnings rate that was paid under specified conditions, and (d) a side-rate consisting of the general wage increases that had occurred since the war.

2. Wage incentives provide workers with a device for directly appropriating part of the benefits of technological improvements and for increasing their earnings without increasing the skill and effort they apply in their work.[28]

Case No. 2. This was illustrated in a plant manufacturing metal containers. In the barrel department, management made

---

[28] It should be pointed out that this aspect of wage incentives is closely related to their use in maintaining the flexibility of labor costs. However, to the extent that wage incentives provide a means for pushing earnings above prevailing market levels, they contribute to excessive costs and thus have a negative impact.

a number of technological improvements in the manufacturing process and, at the same time, loosened piece rates by 12.4 percent. These changes provided workers with a 30 percent increase in their bonus earnings.

Case No. 1. A more detailed account of increasing worker earnings by loosening of standards and improving methods was revealed in a plant fabricating asbestos products. In the spinning department of this plant there had been a gradual increase in average bonus payments. They climbed from 3.2 percent for the week ending January 3, 1942, to 44.1 percent at the end of January, 1945. An investigation to determine the reason for this significant increase in bonus earnings revealed that raw materials had been improved. A cotton core yarn had been added to the roving; hence, its tensile strength was increased greatly. Consequently, the spinning mules produced more yarn. Fewer ends of roving broke in the spinning process. An added reason for the increase in bonus was the fact that the standard for the most common yarn spun was lowered from 90 meters per hour to 75 meters per hour. This yarn accounted for over 70 percent of the department's production. On the other yarns even greater changes were made. The impact of reducing the standard on 10 cut 156 mix yarn from 90 to 75 meters is illustrated by the fact that for the first six months of 1944 the average bonus earned on spinning this yarn was 51 percent. If the old standard of 90 meters per hour had been used, the average bonus would have been 35 percent. Thus, 16 percent of the increase in bonus was attributed to the loosening of the standard.

In summary, this chapter has described the common events and activities observed in the field investigation of this study. It has indicated advantages and disadvantages arising from the use of wage incentives. This empirical evidence, however, fails to provide a basis for generalizing as to the net advantage or disadvantage gained from the use of this device. Before such conclusions may be drawn, it is necessary to reexamine wage incentives in terms of their underlying logic. This task will be undertaken in the following chapter.

III The Theory and Logic of
WAGE INCENTIVES

A REEXAMINATION

The preceding chapter has indicated that the use of wage incentives in actual factory situations may both hinder and promote the attainment of minimum-cost production, and has raised questions as to the causes of these economies and diseconomies. To answer these questions is the task of the present chapter. Accordingly, we shall begin with a consideration of the theory of wage incentives, proceed to an analysis of the logic of their use, and then turn to the implications of this logic under actual operating conditions.

In short, this chapter will examine the implications of wage incentives by the process of analytical reasoning in order to find the logical explanation for the patterns of action observed in the case studies. Once these causal factors are determined, it should be possible to indicate the proper place of wage incentives in the management process and the means for attaining maximum benefit from their use.

THE THEORY OF WAGE INCENTIVES

Wage incentives may be considered in general or in relation to the environment in which they are used. In general, the theory of wage incentives is an example of the theory of economic motivation. Reduced to simple syllogistic form it holds:

That workers work for monetary reward

That for additional remuneration, workers will increase output

That, therefore, a system of pay that automatically ties earnings to output increases production

This logic is sound. In a "free enterprise" system, monetary reward is one of the basic motivations for work. People obtain the means of satisfying their wants and needs by selling productive power to industrial establishments.[1] Money is the principal medium of exchange and the main standard of value. It is not only an accepted measure of and means of control over things material, but it also has intrinsic value as a symbol of status and security.

Furthermore, this logic is consistent with several of the basic moral precepts of our society: (1) that people should be rewarded in accordance with their worth; and (2) that the individual should be "free" to seek his own self-interest. By rewarding extra effort or skill and by increasing the relative freedom of the worker to better his position, wage incentives conform to these basic values.

THE LOGIC OF THE USE OF WAGE INCENTIVES IN THE MANUFACTURING PLANT

The use of wage incentives in the manufacturing plant involves not only their general logic, but also the environment in which they operate. Therefore, before analyzing their use, it is necessary to consider the general nature of the manufacturing plant.

THE NATURE OF THE MANUFACTURING PLANT

The manufacturing plant as an operating unit is a dynamic system involving coordination of the efforts of in-

[1] As used here, productive power includes personal services or the use of property.

dividuals performing a wide variety of specialized tasks. Its component parts are numerous. They consist of individual workers, groups, sections, departments, divisions, and so on.

Each of these is in itself dynamic. Each may change and create a new state within itself. Furthermore, the various parts of the manufacturing plant are mutually related. A change in one aspect or part may cause a change in the relationship of that part to all of the others and a change in the plant as a whole.

The fundamental justification for the manufacturing plant's existence is its contribution to the purposes of the enterprise of which it is a part. In the case of private business enterprise, this purpose is the attainment of profit.[2]

Profit is attained by maintaining revenues in excess of costs.[3] It is a function of a complex of forces. The contribution of the manufacturing plant to the attainment of profits is limited primarily to cost minimization.

The manufacturing plant promotes enterprise profits by minimizing the cost of each unit of output. To achieve this objective, the plant coordinates its component parts and adjusts to technological and economic forces.

The functions involved in this process are: [4]

1. Determination of the organization of the plant. This

---

[2] Cf. Joel Dean: "A business firm is an organization designed to make profits, and profits are the primary measure of its success." *Managerial Economics* (New York, Prentice-Hall, Inc., 1951), p. 3.

[3] There are several definitions of profit. The one used here is the common business concept of revenue exceeding expense as calculated by conventional accounting methods.

[4] The nature of the functions of management has been considered by a number of writers. See Chester I. Barnard, *The Functions of the Executive* (Cambridge, Mass., Harvard University Press, 1938), Chap. XV; E. F. L. Brech, *The Nature and Significance of Management* (2d ed.; London, Sir Isaac Pitman and Sons, Ltd., 1948), p. 30; Neil W. Chamberlain, *The Union Challenge to Management Control* (New York, Harper and Brothers, 1948); and, for an excellent summary of the writings of these and other authors, see Robert Tannenbaum, "The Management Concept: A Rational Synthesis," *The Journal of Business*, XXII, No. 4 (October, 1949), 225–40.

involves determination of the degree and type of specialization of each of the component parts, and establishment of the relations between each part so that they all contribute to the goal of the plant.

2. Translation of the general goal of the plant into meaningful objectives for each of the component parts. The goals of the various specialized units of the plant may not coincide with those of the plant as a whole. Each group or each individual in a group may have specialized purposes or goals; hence, to achieve the over-all purpose of the plant, it is necessary to establish meaningful goals for each unit. These goals must reinforce the attainment of the general objective of the plant.

3. Control of the various component parts of the plant to insure the achievement of their specified tasks. This involves recruiting, selecting, training, and motivating workers, and necessitates the use of budgets, accounting records, and other devices for appraisal of performance.

Given this general nature of the manufacturing plant, it remains to inquire into the ways in which wage incentives may contribute to the achievement of its objective.

THE CONTRIBUTION OF WAGE INCENTIVES TO THE
MANUFACTURING PLANT'S OBJECTIVE

Recalling the unique features of wage incentives (that is, that standards of output are explicitly established and earnings are directly and promptly related by a predetermined formula to the relationship between actual output and standard output), it is apparent that a number of benefits may derive from their use. These are:

1. Wage incentives may be a device for attracting labor. They can result in higher earnings, and thus may be a positive force for attracting labor to the plant.

2. Wage incentives may be helpful in placing workers. They provide a means for differentiating between indi-

vidual workers on the basis of output; hence, they may be used as a guide in placing workers where they will produce most effectively.

3. Wage incentives may direct management's attention to training needs. As a device for focusing attention on worker performance, wage incentives may bring to light worker deficiencies that will point the way to a positive program of training. Moreover, the proper administration of wage incentives involves the careful description of the work method associated with each standard. Such job descriptions may serve to guide the workers toward the use of proper work methods.

4. Wage incentives may induce workers to contribute services at an intensity that promotes the attainment of enterprise purposes. This results from the fact that wage incentives integrate the workers' interest in high earnings with the employer's interest in a high level of output.

5. Wage incentives may result in closer management control of work groups and departments. The standards of performance used under wage incentives provide the basis for budgeting labor costs and checking on actual performance.

6. Wage incentives may encourage management to be thorough in determining the best methods for performing work and in standardizing job conditions. This arises from the need for explicit standards of performance on each job. To be most meaningful, the standard has to be directly related to a given method of performing work; to minimize costs, the standard method should be the most economical.

7. Wage incentives may promote harmonious relations between workers and between the various groups within the plant. By integrating workers' interests, they may help in coordinating the activities of the component parts of the plant. Cooperation may lead to increased output for

all concerned, and, consequently, it may lead to a general increase in earnings. Furthermore, wage incentives may do away with the need for close, driving supervision and thus may provide a basis for more friendly relations between supervisors and workers.

If these are the possible benefits that may come from the use of wage incentives, we must next determine the probability of their attainment. The proper starting point for such an inquiry is consideration of the assumptions implicit in the application of the general wage incentive theory to the manufacturing plant.

APPLICATION OF THE WAGE INCENTIVE THEORY TO MANUFACTURING PLANTS

In its most common form, the general theory of wage incentives as applied to manufacturing plants maintains: Wage incentives stimulate the workers to increase their rates of output and, in so doing, bring about reduced costs and increased profits (or decreased losses).[5]

Implicit in this theory are assumptions concerning the nature of the work, management's ability to set performance standards, the response of rank-and-file factory workers to financial incentives, and the cost structure of the manufacturing plant.

ASSUMPTIONS AS TO THE NATURE OF WORK. For wage incentives to function effectively, a meaningful measure of production must be available. This means that work must be measurable in units that are uniform and distinct. In addition, measurement of output in these units must correlate closely with the skill and effort expended by the worker in maintaining different rates of output.

These requirements imply two things: First, work must

[5] As stated here, the theory of wage incentives concerns only the impact of wage incentives on worker output and its consequent effect on profits. It does not deal with the other possible effects enumerated above (such as improved selection and training).

be standardized. Without standardization of the work, differences in measured output may be caused by variations in job conditions rather than by differences in the worker's diligence and effort. Second, the worker must have a definite and recognized role in determining his own rate of output.[6] If the worker's efforts do not directly influence output, he lacks freedom to influence his earnings, with the result that wage incentives cannot serve as an inducement to increase production.

ASSUMPTIONS AS TO THE SETTING OF STANDARDS OF PERFORMANCE. One of the distinctive features of wage incentives is the fact that standards of performance are explicitly stated for each job or task. For wage incentives to function effectively, it is necessary that these standards of performance be efficiently determined. This means that the standard must not be so high that it will discourage workers from producing or so low that it will result in excessive labor costs. Furthermore, the cost of setting and maintaining standards must not be excessive.

ASSUMPTION OF THE RESPONSE OF RANK-AND-FILE FACTORY WORKERS TO FINANCIAL INCENTIVES. Wage incentives assume that rank-and-file factory workers respond positively to financial incentives, and that this response takes the form of an increased rate of output.

ASSUMPTION AS TO THE COST STRUCTURE OF THE MANUFACTURING PLANT. Implicit in the theory of wage incentives is the assumption that an increased rate of output lowers unit costs. This implies that the plant incurs certain costs that do not increase proportionately with increases in the rate of worker output, and that the increase in the rate of output resulting from the use of wage incentives therefore brings about a reduction in the marginal cost of each incremental increase in output.

---

[6] As used here, "rate of output" refers to the quantity or amount of output produced per unit of time.

IMPLICATIONS OF THE LOGIC OF WAGE INCENTIVES
UNDER OPERATING CONDITIONS

Given these assumptions, what are their implications for the use of wage incentives in the manufacturing plant? Essentially this is determined by the extent to which they apply to the manufacturing situation. Hence, the answer to this question involves consideration of: (1) the extent to which uniform and meaningful measures of production are available; (2) the extent to which standards of performance may be efficiently determined; (3) the extent to which wage incentives motivate workers to increase their rates of output; and (4) the extent to which increases in the rate of worker output will decrease marginal costs.

THE DETERMINATION OF UNIFORM AND MEANINGFUL
MEASURES OF PRODUCTION

The process of manufacturing involves a wide variety of jobs and specialized tasks. For many of these it is possible to measure output in units that actually tend to indicate worker efficiency. However, the plant is a dynamic system existing in a dynamic universe. From time to time every aspect of production processes changes. The amount of change may be small or large. The important fact is that raw materials, machinery, and workers vary from day to day and from hour to hour; hence, jobs may never be completely standardized. It is always possible that variations in measured output may reflect changes in job conditions rather than changes in worker skill or effort.

Furthermore, in most plants there are jobs in which the individual has only a limited amount of freedom in determining his rate of output. Thus, the possibility of measuring work in units that correlate perfectly with worker skill and effort is remote. The best that may be obtained is an approximation; the worst is a complete lack of correspondence between the worker's skill and effort and his measured output.

The implication of the above is that wage incentives should not be applied if work cannot be measured in meaningful units, or if the worker has little or no control over his own output. It follows, then, that in many manufacturing plants there are jobs to which wage incentive systems should not apply.

THE DETERMINATION OF STANDARDS OF PERFORMANCE

Writings in the field give the impression that the efficient determination of standards of performance is to be accomplished by the "science" of time and motion study. Hence, at the outset, it is necessary to consider this approach to rate setting.[7]

F. W. Taylor was the first to popularize the use of time and motion study. He indicated the importance of such studies in the following manner:

Time and motion study are the accurate scientific methods by which the great mass of laws governing the best, easiest and most productive movements of men are investigated. They substitute exact knowledge for prejudiced opinion and force in determining all the conditions of work and pay. . . . As reasonably might we insist on bargaining about the time and place of the rising and the setting sun . . . [as bargain over the results of time and motion study].[8]

This leads to consideration of the question of whether or not motion and time study actually provide for scientific determination of standards of performance. As used here, "scientific" refers to a procedure agreeing with proven laws and resulting in accurate and exact standards.

[7] In this study the terms "rate of output," "rate," "standard of performance," and "standard" are used synonymously.

[8] Frederick W. Taylor, quoted in Robert F. Hoxie, *Scientific Management and Labor* (New York, D. Appleton and Co., 1915), p. 40.

The proper approach to this question is to state clearly the nature of time and motion study, and then, to examine their validity and reliability.

Properly applied, the procedure for setting standards by time and motion study involves the following steps:

1. Studying the methods used to perform the job
2. Determining of the best method for performing the job
3. Standardizing of job conditions and of the method of doing the work
4. Dividing the job into elemental motions
5. Recording the time required for each element
6. Determining the average time for each element (This involves carefully noting all unusual elemental times and explaining the reasons for variations from the average times.)
7. Adjusting the average observed time for each element to establish the time required by a "normal" worker
8. Determining allowances for personal time, unavoidable delays, and fatigue
9. Adding all of the "normal" elemental times and the necessary allowances to get the standard time for the job

To be scientifically valid, the technique of time study must measure what it purports to measure; that is, the quantity of work which a "normal" worker will produce in a given period of time, or, conversely, the length of time required by a "normal" worker to produce a given quantity of work. Thus, in part, the validity of time study rests on the concept of the "normal" worker. This concept has been described in a variety of ways. Carrol describes the requirements of the normal worker as:

The equivalent of effort expected in return for market value of the base rate of pay. It should be the same amount of effort for all types of work, and the variations in the normal skill required should be compensated for by classified base rates.[9]

Barnes defines the normal operator as:

The operator who . . . would possess that amount of skill that would be expected of a man who knew his job well. He should be able to do accurate work, know how to handle his tools, and work to specifications. He would have to be more than a beginner, although he would not be expected to have that super skill which comes only from many years of experience in a special field, or because he is especially well adapted to the particular work. This average operator would be expected to exhibit an average amount of effort or speed. That pace used by operators working without incentive (that is, paid by the day) with reasonably good supervision is what is meant by average effort. The majority of workers should be able to do more than this average.[10]

The point to be emphasized is the vagueness of the criteria used for guiding technicians in the application of time and motion study. The "normal" output of a "normal" or "average" worker is a concept existing only in the mind of the time study man. It is an abstraction which can be applied only in a vague and general way. Thus the validity of time study results can never be precisely and definitely established.

Time study not only lacks a clearly defined goal, it is also of questionable reliability. The same technician timing the same job at different times will frequently develop conflicting standards. Similarly, several technicians studying a given job at the same time often produce varying results.[11]

9 Phil Carrol, Jr., *Time Study for Cost Control* (New York, McGraw-Hill Book Co., Inc., 1943), p. 88.
10 Ralph Barnes, *Motion and Time Study* (New York, John Wiley and Sons, 1940), p. 276.
11 Barnes indicates that it is not uncommon for two trained observers to come up with 15 percent variations in performance standards (*Motion*

The lack of reliability in the results of time study arises from the assumptions implicit in its use. It is assumed that jobs are standardized; that a trained observer can accurately measure the time taken to perform each element of the job; that the time study observer can calculate the correct average time for each element; that he can adjust this average time to represent the average for a "normal" worker; that allowances for fatigue and unavoidable delays can be calculated; and that the total time taken to perform a given job can be determined by adding up average "normal" elemental times and allowances for personal time, unavoidable delays, and fatigue.

Critical analysis of these assumptions indicates that in actual practice time study is little more than a systematic method of guiding judgment. Jobs are seldom standardized. A study taken at one time may not be representative of job conditions at a future date. Human errors enter into the reading of the stop watch. The calculation of a representative sample of observed times involves arbitrary selection of statistical techniques. Leveling (the adjusting of average observed times to represent the time taken by a "normal" worker), is an attempt to use subjective judgment to attain an indefinite goal. Calculation of fatigue allowances involves measurement of phenomenon which, in itself, cannot be objectively defined. Determination of allowances for unavoidable delays assumes that such delays are predictable and that the observations taken are a basis for making that prediction.[12]

and Time Study, p. 277). In the field work of this investigation it was found that standards set by different time study men vary over a wider range. Furthermore, it was noticed that individual time study men tend to develop definite biases in their rate setting.

12 A number of writers have pointed out these weaknesses of the time study technique. See Hoxie, Scientific Management and Labor, pp. 46–47; Ralph Presgrave, The Dynamics of Time Study (2d ed.; New York, McGraw-Hill Book Co. Inc., 1945); William Gomberg, A Trade Union Analysis of Time Study (Chicago, Science Research Associates, 1948); R. S. Uhrbrock,

In summary, analysis of the technique of time study leads to the conclusion that:

> In face of the lack of conformity in methods, lack of clearly defined or explicitly measurable goals, lack of consistency between the results of various engineers, etc., one sees that standard setting is a matter of refined judgment. Ultimately standards are set on the basis of authority not scientific study.[13]

In the absence of a science, the determination of standards is achieved by domination, compromise, or integration.

Determination of standards by domination occurs when one group—either the workers or their supervisors—forces its concept of the correct standard on the other. Frequently the use of such a technique involves a struggle to determine or to test the power of the respective parties.

The use of compromise involves both sides making concessions as to what they will accept as a "correct" rate. Compromise is a method of mutualizing dissatisfaction. At its best it is only a truce, so it tends to break down. The process of compromising on the determination of standards implies an underlying power struggle. Compromise represents a settlement associated with a fear of or appreciation of the cost involved in attempting to set standards by domination.

Integration of the interests of rank-and-file employees and supervisors involves emphasizing the common interests of both parties. It is doubtful that the integration of interests may carry far in setting standards. Wage incentives "put workers into business for themselves." In so doing they divorce the interests of rank-and-file workers

---

A Psychologist Looks at Wage Incentive Methods (New York, American Management Association, 1935); Adam Abruzzi, *Work Measurement* (New York, Columbia University Press, 1952).

13 M. Mundel, *Systematic Time and Motion Study* (New York, Prentice-Hall, Inc., 1947), pp. 155–56.

from management's interests.[14] The worker's interest is to obtain standards that allow high earnings and little physical effort. The limiting factor in pursuit of this interest is the substitution of capital for labor; that is, the point at which labor costs become so excessive that management eliminates the worker's job.

Thus, it appears that setting standards of performance will inevitably be associated with discord. Neither domination nor compromise is a procedure for gaining wholehearted acceptance of standards, and integration of interests tends to have only limited applicability. The very mechanics of wage incentives emphasize fundamental differences between the points of view of rank-and-file workers and management. Hence, it follows that the setting of standards will tend to be a center of conflict and that workers may be expected to use deceit, subterfuge, and economic pressure to forward their own special interests.

WAGE INCENTIVES AS A DEVICE FOR MOTIVATING
WORKERS TO INCREASE THEIR RATE OF OUTPUT

Since the motivation of workers by incentive plans is simply a special aspect of the general problem of motivation, it should be helpful to begin with some generalizations.

MOTIVATION IN GENERAL. Motivation is common to all human activities. It arises from specific needs of individuals. These needs may be biophysical or cultural in origin. Society channels them, provides all sorts of substitutes, and prescribes the socially accepted means of satisfying them.

In a general way, the principal motivations operating in our society arise from the following needs:

1. Biological—such as the need for sustenance, shelter, physical well being

[14] Management is used here to signify those directly responsible to owners.

2. Social—such as the need for approval, status, companionship, feeling of belonging
3. Psychological—such as the desire to be useful, the need to excel, the need for personal power, the need for security, for pride in work, for aesthetic or religious satisfaction

These classes are not totally independent of one another, but they are sufficiently distinct to be useful in this analysis.[15]

Although these needs are common to individuals in our society, their intensities and the means for gratifying them vary from person to person. Each individual develops his own personal pattern of feeling and reacting to his environment. This pattern is uniquely determined by the interrelation of his inherited capacities and his previous and present environment.

Early in life, he learns to act in a manner prescribed by his environment and develops his own patterns of feeling and thinking. These early patterns form a basis for all subsequent learning and give the individual his peculiar, personal, idiomatic way of thinking, acting, and feeling. They create a set which in turn forms the foundation upon which new experiences are integrated into the individual's personality. He shapes, distorts, and otherwise interprets every fact and event to fit his own framework.

This means that the ambitions and needs of each individual tend to be unique. They are to a considerable

[15] See Kimbal Young, *An Introduction to Sociology* (2d ed.; New York, The American Book Company, 1949), pp. 102–4. This classification is not Young's but, in this writer's opinion, is consistent with his concepts. See also L. F. Shaffer, *Psychology of Adjustment* (Boston, Houghton Mifflin Co., 1936), pp. 100–108. Douglas McGregor lists human needs in three categories closely related to the above: physical (food, shelter, rest, etc.), social (the need for companionship, acceptance, etc.), and egoistic (the need for a sense of achievement, self-respect, etc.). "The Supervisor's Job," address before the Management Forum, E. I. du Pont de Nemours and Co., Inc., Wilmington, Delaware, April 16, 1948.

degree predetermined by previous development and inherited capacities. The same activity will mean different things to different individuals, and a given need may be satisfied in a variety of ways by different personalities.

WAGE INCENTIVES AS A MOTIVATING DEVICE. The general logic of wage incentives has already been described. At this point it is desirable to enlarge on the manner in which they may affect worker output, and thus to draw attention to their potential in motivating workers.

In our society, money is a medium of exchange. It is important not only as a means of command over most of the necessities of life, but also because of the distinctions it procures and the status it bestows.[16] Thus, the financial reward offered under wage incentives may be expected to be a positive force in motivating workers.

A second motivational aspect of wage incentives arises from the establishment of an explicit standard of performance. It is a common-sense observation that the mere act of providing a point of reference for evaluating workers' performances will guide them in setting output goals.

[16] Frequently discussions of financial incentives overlook the fact that high-paying jobs tend to symbolize increased status. In many plants opportunity for occupational progress is slight and the drive for status is concentrated on getting more money for doing the same job. Reynolds found this to be true in studying the labor market of New Haven, Conn. He reports:

"To many workers, indeed, more money is virtually the whole meaning of occupational progress. Our first interview schedule contained the question: 'Have you had any promotions since you started work here?' This question had later to be rephrased, because a large proportion of workers answered it by saying, 'Oh yes, I've had three raises since I came with the Company.'

"More money may be obtained in a variety of ways. It may come from plant-wide wage increases. It may come from a gradual loosening up of time standards on an incentive job. . . .

"It is wrong to attribute this drive toward higher earnings simply to a desire for more money to spend. It is due partly to a continuing desire for occupational progress, under conditions in which the only possible evidence of progress is higher earnings." Lloyd George Reynolds, *The Structure of Labor Markets* (New York, Harper and Brothers, 1951), p. 153.

The establishment of explicit, realistic standards of performance provides a means for stimulating workers to high level output.[17]

The importance of standards in motivating workers was experimentally studied by Mace.[18] He found that when the standard of performance was fixed, the subjects did not progress so well as when they were told to do their best. Poorest performance was observed when members of a group were told to aim at surpassing their previous week's record. In investigating to determine why the standards of output were not effective in motivating the group, Mace discovered that the subjects' skill had developed to a level at which they could reasonably expect to reach the standard. Further experiments revealed that by using a moving standard, based on the level of the individual's development and on a general knowledge of the rate of learning for the task, the best results were obtained. Thus, standards of performance were most effective where each standard was adjusted to the level of skill and ability of each individual worker.

The implications of this for the setting of standards under a wage incentive plan are: (1) that the standard may be effective as a pacing device; and (2) that the effectiveness of the standard in bringing forth maximum production will be determined, in part, by the level of effort at which the standard is set. For the more highly skilled or those who work at a more intense pace, the existence of a standard of output which does not challenge their abilities may serve as a brake rather than an accelerator to their production.

Mace's study focuses attention on an important aspect of individual differences (their role in determining re-

---

[17] It should be pointed out that the setting of realistic standards of output may be done independently of wage incentives.

[18] C. A. Mace, *Incentives: Some Experimental Studies*, Industrial Health Research Board, Report No. 72 (Great Britain, 1935).

sponse to a given schedule of output). Another aspect is their importance in determining the response to financial reward.[19] The needs of individuals vary widely. One man's feast can be another man's famine.

Another implication of the general nature of motivation is that a worker's motives may be in conflict. A worker's desire for social approval can clash with his desire to maximize money income. Recent "human relations" literature has focused attention on this conflict. Mayo typifies this trend. He states:

The studies of actual industrial situations which have been carried on show that the desire to stand well with one's fellow, the so-called human instinct of association, easily outweighs merely individual interest and logic of reasoning. . . . The Hawthorne experiment brough out "inconsistencies" of behavior that astonished the engineers and led ultimately to the conclusion that associative instincts overshadowed material conditions as determinants of productivity.[20]

A further implication derived from the nature of worker motivation is that, in some instances, the workers can view wage incentives as punishment for low output, rather than as a positive inducement to increase output. Hence, to

[19] These variations are most noticeable where marked cultural differences exist. See: Allison Davis, "The Motivation of the Underprivileged Worker," in William F. Whyte, ed., *Industry and Society* (New York, McGraw-Hill Book Co., Inc., 1946); Orvis Collins, Melville Dalton, and Donald Roy, "Restriction of Output and Social Cleavage in Industry," *Applied Anthropology*, V, No. 3 (Summer, 1946), 1–14; Melville Dalton, "Worker Response and Social Background," *The Journal of Political Economy*, LV, No. 4 (August, 1947), 323–32.
An interesting subject for further research is the relation of the personality characteristics of workers to their responses to wage incentives. Some work in this area has been done by J. G. Friend and Ernest A. Haggard. Their study was published for the American Psychological Association under the title *Work Adjustment in Relation to Family Background: A Conceptual Basis for Counseling* (Stanford, Stanford University Press, 1948).
[20] Elton Mayo. This quotation has been taken from the loose-leaf digest accompanying *The Social Problems of an Industrial Civilization* (Boston, Harvard University Press, 1945). See also W. B. D. Brown, "Incentives within the Factory," *Occupational Psychology* XIX, No. 2 (April, 1945), 82.

some workers wage incentives can signify a system of penalties rather than one of rewards.

The lack of a definite and precise measure of the correctness of standards has serious implications for the motivation of workers. The first of these is that workers' desires for financial reward or a relaxed work pace may lead them to use pressure and deception to secure loose rates. If this occurs, wage incentives may not actually lead to increased output or decreased costs.

A second inference derived from the problem of setting and maintaining standards is that rates may be of varying looseness; hence, variations in earnings may be more a matter of a worker's luck or trickery than of his increased effort and diligence.[21] If this occurs, the rationality of the wage payment system is weakened and its impact in motivating workers is reduced.

A further implication of the problem of setting standards is that the varying tightness and looseness of rates injects a dynamic element into the plant earning structure. Traditional earnings differentials are distorted. The plant status quo is upset and the following tendencies develop:

1. Workers refuse to accept promotions to more skilled jobs that do not provide a greater earnings potential.

2. Workers on jobs with low earnings potentials apply pressure for the relaxation of standards.

3. Friction tends to develop between nonincentive workers and incentive workers, and between high-earnings and low-earnings groups.

4. Nonincentive workers bring pressure to bear for the application of wage incentives to their work.

These actions are directly related to the psychological and sociological motivations of workers.

21 This tendency has been noted by Norah Davis in "Some Psychological Effects on Women Workers of Payment by the Individual Bonus Method," *Occupational Psychology* XVIII, No. 2 (April, 1944), 53–62.

Finally, the problem of setting and maintaining standards of output enhances workers' fears of rate cuts and thus encourages ceilings on output. In tenure employment, the desire for financial reward is seldom approached from a short-run point of view. The workers are interested in maximum income over a sustained period of time. They recognize that unusual or exceptional earnings will stimulate management to change methods and to apply new standards. Hence, to maximize their long-run income, the workers establish and police ceilings on production.

In summary, wage incentives may work in a positive or negative manner. They release forces that may increase worker motivation. However, the paradoxical nature of worker motives and the problems associated with setting and maintaining standards of output tend to offset this response.

EFFECT OF INCREASED OUTPUT ON MARGINAL COST

One of the assumptions implied in the theory of wage incentives is that the increased output stimulated by a system of payment geared to results will bring about decreased unit costs and increased profits. Whether or not these results will be forthcoming depends upon the impact of wage incentives on marginal costs and on the nature of the demand for the firm's product.[22]

A case will serve to illustrate this. If it is assumed that a firm produces one item, that the demand for the item is perfectly inelastic (that is, the same quantity will be demanded at any price), that there is no substitution of

[22] In this discussion, it is assumed that the wage incentive used rewards workers in proportion to their increase in output. For example: If workers increase output 10 percent over standard, they receive a 10 percent increase in earnings.

If the standard of output is above the level of past performance, the wage incentive plan will result in a direct decrease in direct labor costs. (Here it is assumed that workers produce at standard efficiency or better.)

If the wage incentive is a sharing plan, such as the Rowan or the Halsey, management will automatically share in any savings in direct labor cost.

labor for capital, and that wage incentives cause the workers to increase their rate of output, then to produce the given output the firm will require fewer workers.

With the total output of the firm constant, the possibility of reducing total unit costs by spreading fixed and semifixed costs to a greater number of units is ruled out. The only savings derived from the increased rate of output will be those brought about by the reduction in the size of the firm's labor force (for example, such items as vacation pay, holiday pay, pension costs, and health insurance will be reduced). However, offsetting these would be the increase in costs associated with administering the wage incentive system—increased work-in-process inventories, more complicated and detailed accounting records, more grievances over standards, and so on. Hence, under the artificial circumstances that have been assumed, the net benefits credited to the use of wage incentives may be slight.

In actual practice the conditions assumed do not hold. Increased efficiency in the use of labor will tend to result in an increase in the volume of the plant's production. Hence, it tends to spread fixed and semifixed costs and to decrease total unit costs.[23] If fixed costs per unit are large, the benefit of increased output may be significant.

Thus, the assumption that increased output will lead to increased profits (or decreased losses) is primarily valid. It represents the prevailing tendency that exists in most modern factories. The degree to which it is realized depends on: (1) the amount of increase in production; (2) the relation of fixed and semifixed costs to total unit cost; (3)

[23] All of this may be simply stated in economic terms: The increase in the rate of output will lead to a reduction in marginal costs. Hence, if the demand for the firm's product is elastic, the firm will reach a new equilibrium position with a greater volume of production; and if the elasticity of demand for the firm's product is greater than unity, the firm's profits will increase (as used here "profits" refers to the accountant's concept of revenues exceeding costs).

the costs incurred in installing and administering the wage incentive system; and (4) the elasticity of the demand for the firm's products.

In summary: The worker motivation theory of wage incentives, when applied to factory work, holds that under specified assumptions wage incentives motivate workers to increase their rate of output and, in so doing, bring about lower unit costs and a resulting increase in the firm's profits (or decrease of its losses). When analyzed in terms of its underlying assumptions, the theory proves to be consistent and valid; that is, if work is measurable, if the units of measurement are such that there is a direct causal relationship between worker effort and diligence and measured output, if standards of production can be efficiently determined and maintained, if workers are motivated to maximize their monetary income, and if the firm can reduce unit costs by increasing worker output, then wage incentives will contribute to maximizing profits (or minimizing losses).

However, analysis of these assumptions indicates that they are not descriptive of all of the real world. Not all work can be measured in units which relate worker effort to output. Often standards of performance are set by the use of power and persuasion. Workers' motives can conflict. Workers' responses to financial reward may encourage them to falsify production records, mislead time study men, and bargain for loose standards. In short, the worker motivation theory of wage incentives is limited in its application to the payment of rank-and-file workers in manufacturing plants.

WAGE INCENTIVES AS A DEVICE FOR STIMULATING
MANAGEMENT TO BE MORE EFFICIENT

It has previously been indicated that there are two theories justifying the use of wage incentives. The worker motivation theory has been considered in the preceding section. It remains to analyze the management efficiency theory.

Actually these are not separate and distinct. The latter includes the former. The separation of the two is simply an aid to analysis. It distinguishes the main concepts emphasized by writers and practitioners.

The management efficiency theory holds that wage incentives not only directly motivate workers but also stimulate management to be more efficient in performing many of its functions, such as determining the best methods of work; standardizing job conditions; setting performance standards; selecting, placing, and training workers; planning and scheduling production; and building teamwork.

Implicit in this theory are two basic assumptions: (1) that under normal operating conditions management is relatively inefficient, and (2) that wage incentives will actually stimulate management to do a better job.

It is obvious that if management is functioning efficiently it has little to gain from the use of wage incentives. However, in actual practice plants seldom reach perfection. Some improvement is always possible. The point to be emphasized is that the potential gain in this area is inversely related to the existing level of management efficiency. The poorer the management, the greater the potential improvement.[24]

The general nature of the management incentive theory of wage incentives has been indicated.[25] It remains to analyze the impact of wage incentives with respect to setting standards of performance; determining the best method of doing work; planning and scheduling production; and

---

[24] A corollary to this statement it that these plants (the inefficiently managed) are precisely those that are most likely to be unsuccessful in administering wage incentives. Hence, wage incentives are most needed where they are least likely to succeed.

[25] See pp. 75–77 above.

recruiting, selecting, and training workers and building teamwork.

THE IMPACT OF WAGE INCENTIVES ON THE DETERMINA-TION OF PERFORMANCE STANDARDS. One of the essential jobs of management is the establishment of standards of performance. Such standards serve as a guide for planning and a basis for evaluating performance.

The management motivation theory holds that the use of wage incentives forces management to do a better job of setting standards, because standards of performance are essential to a wage incentive plan, and they are explicitly related to worker earnings. Hence, it is argued that under wage incentives standards must be set, and they must be set correctly.

There can be no doubt that the use of wage incentives focuses attention on the establishment of performance standards. However, there are reasons to believe that it also tends to inject bias into these standards.

This follows from the fact that there is no final and absolute way in which to judge the accuracy of standards. Standards work because workers make them work.[26] If workers do not accept a standard, they may apply a variety of techniques to have it changed (such as slowdowns, strikes, and sabotage). Thus, if management sets tight standards of output, the workers may agitate to have the

[26] This fact has been pointed out by numerous students. For example, Mundel says, "Many standard times function well, even though they are incorrect, because the workers have learned that it is advantageous to have them function." *Systematic Time and Motion Study*, p. 156.

Ralph Presgrave, William Whyte, Clinton Golden, and Harold Ruttenberg have pointed out that (1) many standards may be in error by plus or minus 50 percent; (2) numerous worker grievances are for relaxation of standards; and (3) rechecking of standards reveals that many of them are in error. C. Golden and H. Ruttenberg, *The Dynamics of Industrial Democracy* (New York, Harper and Brothers, 1942); Presgrave, *Dynamics of Time Study;* William F. Whyte, "Incentives for Productivity: The Bundy Tubing Case," *Applied Anthropology* (now *Human Organization*), Vol. VII (Spring, 1948), and included in *Human Factors in Management* (rev. ed.; New York, Harper and Brothers, 1951), ed. by S. D. Hoslett.

rates liberalized. However, if management sets loose rates, it is unlikely that pressures will be exerted to correct the situation. In such instances, it is probable that the workers will set ceilings on production to prevent management from learning of the looseness of its rates. In this manner, under wage incentives, an upward bias (that is, a tendency toward loose standards) is injected into rate setting.

The special interests of the lower-level supervision may reinforce this bias. Foremen tend to be judged by the bonus earnings of their subordinates. The foreman knows that any sudden or significant change in the level of bonus earned in his department will bring about an investigation by his superiors. Hence the foreman's interest is in relatively consistent bonus earnings for his men. One of the easiest ways for him to achieve this end is to secure reasonably loose standards of output and then to enforce ceilings on earnings. This means that when work is flowing smoothly, the rank-and-file workers will maintain a relaxed pace and will significantly restrict output. However, if unusual delays arise, the workers will still be able to maintain their average earnings without undue effort.

THE IMPACT OF WAGE INCENTIVES ON DETERMINATION OF WORK METHODS. Before a performance standard may be set, a definite method for doing the work must be established. The question to be answered is: "Do wage incentives stimulate management to do a better job in determining work methods?"

Although a categorical answer to this question can not be given, several significant tendencies are noticeable. On the positive side is the fact that if management is to do a good job of setting standards, it must first thoroughly study methods. Hence, in the sense that wage incentives focus attention on methods of work, it can be argued that wage incentives stimulate management to improve work methods.

However, the effectiveness of wage incentives must be judged in terms of a definite point of reference. Probably the most realistic comparison to make is between a motion study program under wage incentives and one under a time wage system. When analyzed in this context, it becomes apparent that wage incentives create self-limiting forces.

First, wage incentives develop pressures for rapid standard setting. One of the dilemmas of administering wage incentives is determination of how long a new job should run before a standard of performance is established. Until a standard is set, the workers will slow down. They will restrict production in order to encourage the setting of a liberal standard. The excessive labor costs arising from such a situation tempt management to apply pressure on the time study men to rate new jobs rapidly. Furthermore, if the workers suffer a loss in earnings while working on an unrated job, added pressure will be applied.

Thus, on a new job, pressure tends to be exerted to install rates before the job is running smoothly. The time study men need not be too concerned about this fact. They may protect themselves from errors by guaranteeing standards only so long as the method of doing the job is unchanged. Hence, if a loose rate develops, the time study men usually have the excuse that the method was changed.[27]

A further complication is that wage incentives increase the probability that method changes will lead to friction and unrest. When a method is changed, "proper" standards of performance must be set for the new job. Conflicting values as to what is proper lead to costly grievances.

[27] One of the patterns observed in interviews with industrial engineers was the tendency to blame loose rates on the foremen. The common statement was: "Loose rates arose from poor foremanship. Foremen failed to report method changes; hence, the precedent of applying the old rate was established."

The workers generally use past output as a basis of comparison in determining the "proper" rate. They reason that their pay per unit of output should not be reduced. On the other hand, management argues that worker effort and skill should determine the rate. For example: If management installs a new machine that doubles the worker's rate of output without requiring increased skill or effort on his part, management will maintain that the worker's earnings on the new job should be no greater than they were with the old method. The worker may argue that he is doubling his output and should therefore receive double the pay. The worker tends to label any standard which falls short of this a "rate cut."

In actual practice the worker may accept less than double earnings, but the fact remains that a difference of opinion over standards usually exists. The wage incentive system intensifies this difference by directly relating it to the worker's money income.

The friction encountered in making methods improvements on wage incentive jobs tends to discourage management from making all but the most dramatic and profitable changes. In other words, wage incentives increase the cost of change and make it uneconomical for management to make innovations that might be profitable under a time-wage system.

A further limitation of wage incentives as a device for stimulating the development of the best work method arises from the usual guarantee that "rates will remain unchanged so long as methods are constant." To the worker this implies that any method improvement he devises may lead to a cut in his rate. Thus, the self-interest of the worker discourages him from suggesting major improvements.[28]

[28] To overcome this weakness some companies establish special systems to encourage rank-and-file workers to make suggestions. Usually such "sug-

Frequently the workers do improve job methods, but the fear of a rate cut may cause them to use numerous ruses to prevent the industrial engineers from learning of the change (for example, they restrict output, hide special tools in their lockers, and the like). Thus, wage incentives tend to prevent the plant from obtaining the full benefit of the worker's knowledge.

Wage incentives may also lead management to make "uneconomical" methods changes. This occurs where loose rates have resulted in exorbitant earnings. In order to restore order to the hierarchy of earnings and eliminate excessive labor costs, management may initiate methods changes aimed at justifying a rate cut rather than increasing output. Such methods changes are uneconomical in the sense that they would not have been worth while prior to the establishment of wage incentives.

Thus, it appears that management will gain more from a consciously planned program of work simplification and methods improvement under a time rate system of remuneration than it will when such a program is tied to the administration of wage incentives. The very use of wage incentives tends to set into motion forces which limit the development of the most efficient methods of work.

WAGE INCENTIVES AS A DEVICE FOR AIDING MANAGEMENT TO PLAN AND SCHEDULE PRODUCTION. In the usual manufacturing plant, with its division of labor and specialization of operations, the coordination of production in-

---

gestion plans" are administered by a special committee which reviews the suggestions for methods improvement submitted by the workers and then decides on a monetary reward for each cost-saving suggestion that is adopted.

The field studies of this investigation indicated that unless such suggestion plans are accompanied by a high-pressure propaganda campaign they tend to cause more trouble than they are worth. The difficulties center on the questions: Has the person making the suggestion really originated it? Is the reward for a good suggestion adequate or fair? and Why is the processing of suggestions so time consuming?

volves detailed scheduling, dispatching, and follow-up. To minimize costs, management must maintain minimum inventories and at the same time have adequate supplies on hand.

It is argued that wage incentives contribute to management's success in performing these functions by: (1) supplying management with the detailed information required for proper scheduling of production, (2) bringing into focus any unusual variations in job conditions, and (3) encouraging "optimum" output.

Wage incentives as a source of scheduling information. If wage incentives are to function, explicit standards of output must be stated and comparisons must be made between standard output and actual output. Hence, as a result of the use of wage incentives, management develops an administrative point of reference for scheduling production and for evaluating performance.[29]

Wage incentives as a device for bringing into focus serious variations from standard conditions. Standards of performance are predicated upon reasonably standard working conditions. If there are sudden and wide variations from standard conditions, rates become exceptionally tight or loose. From this it is reasoned that wage incentives will automatically bring to management's attention significant deviations from standard conditions.

Here again a bias arises. Workers will complain only about those changes which limit their rate of output (and hence decrease their earnings). For example, they will file grievances over loss of earnings arising from such events as machine breakdowns, lack of raw materials, and poor quality of raw materials, but they will seldom call to management's attention changes that facilitate production. In fact, if such changes do occur the workers tend to ap-

---

[29] It should be pointed out that this procedure can also exist independent of wage incentives.

propriate the benefits by relaxing their work pace and/or slightly increasing their output. Seldom do they respond by significantly increasing their rates of output.[30]

Wage incentives as a device for encouraging "optimum" output. One of the problems in understanding wage incentives arises from a failure to differentiate between the "maximum" output of workers and their "optimum" output. Many writers imply that workers should always release their maximum effort and skill to produce as rapidly as possible on every job. In actuality, what is necessary for efficient production is that workers be encouraged to work at an "optimum" rate. Here "optimum" refers to the highest rate of worker output that is consistent with coordination of the outputs of the plant's component parts.

The difference between "optimum" and "maximum" output becomes apparent in situations where significant variations in work conditions occur. If the worker maximizes his output, his performance will closely correlate with changes in job conditions. The worker's rate of output will vary widely. The frequent fluctuations will tend to disrupt schedules and to necessitate excessive work-in-process inventories.

In contrast, if the worker maintains an "optimum" rate of output, he will produce at a rate which facilitates the smooth flow of materials through the manufacturing processes. The optimum output of the individual worker is at a level consistent with the smooth coordination of mutually related jobs. The point to be emphasized is that the optimum output includes a concept of steady and predictable performance.

Wage incentives function to promote optimum output. They provide workers with explicit points of reference in setting production targets and provide workers with spe-

[30] For the logic supporting the maintenance of ceilings on output, see pp. 41–43, above.

cific goals. The manner in which this occurs had been described in the section dealing with ceilings on output.[31]

Many writers fail to see the importance of ceilings on output. They imply that this phenomenon is ipso facto undesirable. The weakness of such logic is obvious. Without some sort of ceiling on output, the usual manufacturing plant would find planning and scheduling an extremely difficult and costly task. Day-to-day variations in the same worker, between workers, in raw materials, and in machines would tend to disrupt production schedules.

Thus, in the usual manufacturing plant, with its specialization and division of labor, it is apparent that ceilings on output encouraged by the use of wage incentives may serve a useful function. They may allow closer scheduling and better coordination of the production processes.

The net benefit that may be attributed to wage incentives in this stabilizing of rates of output is hard to evaluate. It depends on (1) the level of output at which ceilings are set, (2) the degree to which workers can maintain earnings by subterfuge or special allowances, and (3) the extent to which workers build up "kitties" of unreported production.

If standards are so loose that ceiling on output are set at a level that leaves workers with excessive idle time, the loss due to excessive labor costs may offset the gain arising from a more predictable rate of output. In addition, if workers maintain their earnings at a relatively stable level by cheating or winning special allowances, the actual level of output will not be constant. Furthermore, if workers build up excessive inventories of semiprocessed parts ("kitties"), the relatively stable rates of production as reported through the wage incentive system will be a fiction.

In summary, a central problem in plant management is the coordination of the various mutually related parts

[31] See pp. 41–43, above.

of the operating unit. This is facilitated by "optimum" production. Wage incentives, by encouraging ceilings on output, contribute to the stability and predictability of production. The degree to which this results in optimum production depends on the level of worker efficiency at which ceilings are set and the extent to which workers' earnings correlate with their actual rates of output.

THE IMPACT OF WAGE INCENTIVES ON PERSONNEL MANAGEMENT. One of the justifications for the use of wage incentives is that they aid management in dealing with rank-and-file personnel. This has been suggested by numerous writers and practitioners. The points of emphasis vary. The general tenor of the remarks may be discussed in terms of the impact of wage incentives on recruitment, selection, placement, and training of workers, and on co-operative relations in the plant.

Wage incentives as a device for attracting and holding workers. It is pointed out that earnings are higher under wage incentives than they are under time wage systems.[32] Hence, it is argued that wage incentives are a device for attracting and holding workers. The assumptions implied in this reasoning are that (1) workers know of the earnings on alternative jobs, and (2) workers are attracted to those jobs providing the greatest earnings.

The importance of wages in attracting labor has been the subject of numerous empirical studies.[33] The general consensus of their findings is:

[32] See pp. 22-24, above.

[33] As examples of such studies, see W. Rupert Malaurin and Charles A. Myers, "Wages and the Movement of Factory Labor," *The Quarterly Journal of Economics,* LVII (February, 1943), 241-64; Lloyd George Reynolds and Joseph Shister, *Job Horizons* (New York, Harper and Brothers, 1948), Chaps. III and IV, pp. 84, 87-88; E. Wight Bakke, *The Unemployed Worker* (New Haven, Yale University Press, 1940), pp. 165-252; Reynolds, *Structure of Labor Markets,* Chaps. VIII and IX; Charles A. Myers and George P. Shultz, *The Dynamics of a Labor Market* (New York, Prentice-Hall, Inc., 1951), Chap. IV.

1. Rank-and-file workers seldom have detailed knowledge of job opportunities. Friends and relatives are the principal sources of information.

2. Rank-and-file workers seldom systematically canvass the market. They have only fragmentary information about job openings, rates of pay, and the like.

3. Most moves to new jobs are forced by layoffs or discharges.

4. Only in the case of voluntary job movement is there a trend toward the higher-wage firms.

The inference to be drawn from existing field research is that wages are not of major importance in attracting labor to a given firm. Only when frequent voluntary job movements exist will high wages be a significant factor in recruiting rank-and-file employees.

The role of wages in holding employees on given employment has been a subject of controversy. Numerous attitude surveys have been made to determine the relative rank of wages in contributing to the worker's job satisfaction. The findings of such studies generally reveal that wages rank relatively low (from third to seventh).[34]

It is questionable whether these surveys contribute to an understanding of the role of wages in reducing turnover. Job satisfaction is not composed of many separate elements. It is an alloy. To ask which is more important

---

[34] For example: A study made in 1935 by Hoppock and Spiegler revealed that in a small work group the factors most frequently mentioned as important to job satisfaction were, in order of importance: (1) work associates, (2) the work itself, (3) the boss, (4) variety, (5) freedom in work, (6) hours, and (7) earnings. R. Hoppock and S. Spiegler, "Job Satisfaction," *Occupations, The Vocational Guidance Magazine,* XVI (1938), 636–43. Also see: R. B. Hersey, "Psychology of Workers," *Personnel Journal,* XIV (1936), 291–96; National Industrial Conference Board, *Factors Affecting Employee Morale,* in *Studies in Personnel Policy,* No. 85 (1947); Lawrence G. Lindahl, "What Makes a Good Job?" *Personnel,* XXV (January, 1949), 263–66; M. L. Blum and J. J. Russ, "A Study of Employee Attitudes toward Various Incentives," *Personnel,* XIX (1942), 438–44; Clifford Jurgensen, "Selected Factors Which Influence Job Performance," *Journal of Applied Psychology,* XXXI (1937), 553–64.

to the worker—human relations on the job (independence, fairness of treatment, and the like), the intrinsic nature of the job (skills, variety, conditions of work, and the like), or wages—is like asking which leg of a three-legged stool is most important. The factors entering into job satisfaction are not separate and independent. They exist in a system of mutual causality, a system in which everything depends on everything else.

Despite the empirical evidence that, generally, wages are unimportant in attracting labor, experience in the Second World War indicated that in a tight labor market relative wages are important. During this period many firms adopted wage incentives as a means of circumventing wage stabilization regulations.[35] By setting loose standards and granting liberal allowances, these plants significantly increased the earnings of their workers.[36]

In summary, there is little evidence that the high earnings associated with wage incentives will always be effective in attracting and holding rank-and-file factory work-

[35] In July, 1942, the National War Labor Board announced its policy of stabilizing wages. It publicized its Little Steel Formula providing that wages were stabilized at a level 15 percent above that of January 1, 1941. On October 3, 1942, Executive Order No. 9250 was issued. It provided that: "The National War Labor Board shall not approve any increase in the wage rates prevailing on September 15, 1942, unless such increase is necessary to correct maladjustments or inequalities, to eliminate substandards of living, to correct gross inequities, or to aid in the effective prosecution of the war." Steel Case Research Committee of the Steel Industry, *Steel Wages, a National Issue* (April, 1944), pp. 5, 8.

[36] The only wage control over the operation of an existing incentive plan was the general requirement that, with changes in products or methods, new standards must be set "in line" with existing rates. This control breaks down under conditions comparable to those of World War II. Such things as increased product runs and more standardized products contributed to increased output. Such conditions also created the opportunity for a general loosening of production standards. "That this loosening of production standards took place quite extensively in the piece rate industries and in other incentive operations during World War II is hardly open to serious debate." E. Robert Livernash, "Stabilization of the Internal Wage Rate Structure," *Industrial and Labor Relations Review*, VII (January, 1954), 216.

ers. However, under special conditions, such as those existing in the labor market of the Second World War, there
is reason to believe that wage incentives may be important
in recruiting labor and reducing turnover.[37]

*The impact of wage incentives on selection and place-
ment of workers.* One of the important management problems arising from the existence of individual differences
and specialization is the placing of individuals on jobs
that are compatible with their abilities, interests, and ambitions. With respect to this, the job of management is to
differentiate among workers so as to place each individual
in the job that will allow him to make his greatest contribution to enterprise profits.

Worker contributions to enterprise profit are of two
types.[38]

1. Minimizing the cost of producing a given output.
This involves economizing in the use of the materials,
equipment, and the worker's time.

2. Coordinating the component parts of the manufacturing plant. That is, the worker's contribution to cooperative relationships within the plant.

Wage incentives are one of the devices used by management for differentiating between workers. They are a
means of directly discriminating between workers on the
basis of output. They automatically relate earnings to
operator efficiency as judged by an explicit standard of

[37] In the cases covered by this investigation there was a noticeable
tendency for wage incentives to result in evasion of wage stabilization regulations. However, it should be pointed out that not all of the managements
were fully conscious of what they were doing. Frequently they reported, and
evidence bore them out, that they settled each wage incentive grievance on
an ad hoc basis. The primary explanation for deterioration of standards
lies in the general economic forces operating during the World War II
labor market. The firms were more interested in getting out the production
than in cutting costs. The excess profits tax and cost plus contracts encouraged this attitude. Furthermore, the acute scarcity of labor provided
workers with increased power in bargaining over standards.

[38] T. L. Whisler, Merit Rating: A Management Tool (unpublished Ph.D.
dissertation, University of Chicago, School of Business, March, 1953), p. 79.

performance. Thus, they are an aid in identifying the strongly motivated workers. In so doing, they focus management attention on variations in performance and provide management with a guide for promoting, transferring, demoting, and discharging workers.[39]

However, there are limitations implied by the preceding discussion:

1. The appropriateness of differentiations resulting from the use of wage incentives will be limited by the accuracy of the standard used in determining worker efficiency. The tendency for standards to be inconsistent and inaccurate (as judged by the relationship of skill and effort to earnings) implies that differences in workers' earnings may be caused by weaknesses in setting correct standards rather than differences in the diligence and effort of the various individuals.

2. Differentiation among workers on the basis of wage incentive earnings is not a complete measure of their respective contributions to enterprise profits. It fails to consider the worker's contribution to the coordination of the plant's various activities. In fact, the individuals earning the most, the "rate busters," tend to detract from harmonious relations between workers. Frequently, rate busters cause so much friction that it is unrealistic to judge them solely in terms of their output.

These weaknesses in the use of wage incentives as a means of differentiating between workers lead to the conclusion that, although they may be helpful in this process, they should always be supplemented by other devices, and should never be considered completely reliable.

The impact of wage incentives on the training of rank-and-file workers. Wage incentives may be effective in bringing to light training needs. For example: If one or two

[39] A few of the other devices used for selecting and placing workers are interviews, merit ratings, and work tests.

workers in a work group consistently fall below the expected rate of output, their low earnings record under the wage incentive system may prompt management to investigate. The investigation may reveal a training problem rather than tight standards or lack of motivation.

In addition, the mechanics of administering wage incentives usually provide workers with detailed information on the proper method of performing the work. The description of the work method may serve as a job instruction device.

The impact of wage incentives on cooperative relations in the plant. At the rank-and-file level, wage incentives produce both desirable and undesirable effects on cooperation. On the positive side, they may integrate the interests of workers by focusing their attention on the increased earnings that result from cooperating to attain increased output.

On the negative side are numerous problems growing out of the difficulties surrounding the setting and maintaining of accurate and consistent standards of performance. Pigors and Myers have indicated the general nature of this problem. They point out: "Wage differentials are a mark of social status in the factory organization. If they do not correspond with the relative significance of jobs as employees view them, the workers' sense of justice is outraged." [40]

Illogical and dynamic variations in earnings injected into the plant wage structure by wage incentives tend to engender serious enmities among workers. Jobs that normally rate low in status may pay better than the traditionally "good" jobs. Hence, workers holding the "good" jobs may feel that established differentials should be restored. They will apply pressure to have management loosen

---

[40] P. Pigors and C. Myers, *Personnel Administration* (2d ed.; New York, McGraw-Hill Book Co., Inc., 1950), p. 255.

standards. If this fails, they may request transfers to the better-paying work. Since the workers holding the low-status (but high-paying) jobs tend to resent being displaced, personal hostilities develop.

A second manner in which wage incentives contribute to undesirable personal relations is illustrated when groups of workers push their earnings above established ceilings. Under such conditions, workers on auxiliary jobs who are unable to secure similar increases in earnings may argue that their job duties have been increased by the increase in the production of the other workers. Such arguments result in bickering over the precise limits of job duties and the development of personal antagonism among workers.

A third implication of the use of wage incentives is that the workers who are unable to earn a bonus will argue for liberal wage incentive plans. They will expect other workers to support them in applying pressure to gain this end. For example: If the indirect workers are paid time wages and the direct workers are under a wage incentive system, the traditional relationship between the earnings of the indirect workers and the direct workers will be changed. The indirect workers will apply pressure to restore the previous relationship. If the direct workers do not actively support this action, conflict between the two groups will develop.

Further interpersonal conflict may result if some workers ignore established ceilings on output. The work group's fear that unlimited output will lead to unemployment, rate cutting, or tighter standards on new work causes it to apply pressure to "rate busters." This pressure may vary from social ostracism to sabotage. It does not contribute to healthy cooperation.

If there is an industrial union in the manufacturing plant, it appears that the negative impact of wage incentives will be enhanced. The very organization and structure of the union contributes to distortion of the wage structure.

In a general sense, the organization of the industrial union parallels the hierarchy of plant management: at the foreman level are stewards; at the plant superintendent level are local union officers; and at this level and above are the paid representatives of the national or international union. At the plant level, one of the major functions of the union is to challenge managerial decisions. The organization of the union is designed to perform this function.

The local union is essentially a political organization. In theory, if not in practice, the election of officers is based on popular support of the members. Moreover, the high rate of turnover of local officers revealed by this investigation emphasizes their lack of absolute power. They maintain their positions in the union by winning the support of the rank-and-file members. Hence, local union officers approach grievances over wage incentives as political matters, using them as a means of winning support of the rank-and-file members. Hence, their first reaction to workers' complaints is to "try to get something extra for the boys."

The lack of precise and uniform criteria for judging standards provides local union leaders with ample opportunity to influence rates. The net result is an array of standards set by power or persuasion rather than more systematic means. Both the friction associated with wage rate grievances and the distortion of the earnings structure resulting from inequities in the political pressures applied to union leaders tend to disrupt effective cooperative relations in the plant.[41]

41 For an excellent discussion of the implications of wage incentives to industrial unions, see Leonard R. Sayles, "The Impact of Incentives on

At the lower level of line supervision, wage incentives have an interesting impact. Many foremen are in favor of the use of wage incentives, because "wage incentives do away with the need for driving supervision."

Analysis reveals additional reasons why foremen support the use of wage incentives. First, the production records, as revealed by the operation of the wage incentive system, reflect on the foreman. If he can secure fairly loose rates for his department, he is in a position to make a favorable showing for his superiors.

Another reason for the foreman to favor wage incentives arises from the fact that they are a device for gaining co-operation from subordinates. Wage incentives provide the foreman with numerous situations in which he may demonstrate his loyalty to his subordinates; for example, he may help to gain liberal standards of performance, he may condone falsification of production records, and he may grant special allowances to help workers maintain consistent earnings.[42]

A final reason why the foreman may favor wage incentives arises from the fact that under an incentive plan his responsibility for determining standards of performance may be delegated to the industrial engineering department. Thus, the foreman is protected from his subordinates' accusations that rates are too tight and from his superiors' accusations that rates are too liberal. The operation of the wage incentive plan provides the foreman with a scapegoat. It allows him to evade authority for one of his most difficult jobs—the determination of standards of performance.

Although wage incentives frequently have the support

Inter-Group Work Relations: A Management and Union Problem," *Personnel* (May, 1952), pp. 483–90.

[42] It should be pointed out that the degree to which a foreman may use wage incentives in this manner depends upon the system of controls exercised by his superiors.

of foremen, it is apparent that this support may ignore the needs of the plant as a whole. Inherent in the use of wage incentives are forces which tend to limit the effectiveness of lower-level supervision. These forces work quite subtly, and often they are not fully recognized.

The first of these arises from the tendency for the authority of lower-level supervisors to be changed. The staff departments, whose correct duties are to advise, educate, and inspect, gradually take over the functions of line supervisors. In so doing they violate a basic principle of management: Line management must retain the full authority to carry out the function for which it is held responsible. It cannot successfully delegate this authority.[43]

The production and sale of goods at a profit involves the integration and direction of specialized human activities. This is the function of line management. The separation of the function of assigning work to people and the settling of problems arising in getting this work out leads to an impossible situation. For example, giving the industrial engineers authority to settle grievances over working conditions and standards of performance in effect gives authority to those who are not directly charged with responsibility. Giving this authority to staff specialists undermines the line supervisor's control. The difficulties that arise impede the integrative activity that is the principal function of line management.

The second limiting force is closely related to the first. It concerns the fact that top management generally forbids lower-level supervisors to make deviations from stated wage incentive policies. This fact, plus the tendency for staff personnel to assume line authority, forces lower-level supervisory employees (foremen, department bosses, and so forth) to be overly cautious in administering wage in-

---

[43] For a clear statement of the proper role of line and staff personnel, see Pigors and Myers, *Personnel,* Chap. II.

centives. They refrain from "sticking their necks out."
They attempt to save face by avoiding the embarrassing
experience of being reversed on decisions. They tend to
refer all administrative questions either to the staff department or to higher levels of management. The net result of
this is a tendency for lower-level supervisors to abdicate
their positions of authority for the work of their subordinates. Foremen tend to become nothing more than glori-
fied errand boys.

Thus the use of wage incentives may undermine the
effectiveness of lower-level supervision. It tends to do so by
bringing about a separation of authority and responsibility
and by narrowly circumscribing the range of the decisions
that the supervisors may make without the threat of review and reversal by higher authorities.

IV Understanding the Use of
WAGE INCENTIVES

Evidence that wage incentives may have a net positive or
negative impact on plant efficiency leads to the question
of how a plant may insure optimum benefits from their
use. Consideration of this question directs attention to the
complexity of the manufacturing plant's operation. It is
a complicated system of mutually related parts. These parts
act, react, and interact to create and maintain the "whole"
which, in turn, simultaneously patterns the activities of the
parts. For example: the usual manufacturing plant is composed of individuals, sections, gangs, departments, and divisions. The activities of the individuals composing each
specific section are in part determined by the nature of
that section as a whole and in part by the nature of the
specific individuals composing each respective section. In
other words, the various "parts" of a given plant both
determine, and are determined by, the nature of the plant
as a whole.[1]

This concept of the manufacturing plant implies that
simple cause-and-effect ad hoc thinking has only limited
value in considering specific operating problems. Each
part and its functioning is one aspect or dimension within
a complex of many dimensions. The whole is not a super-

---

[1] This concept of the nature of the manufacturing plant is to be compared with the development of the field concept in physics. Attention is
focused upon the field in which events occur and the interrelations among
particles and events which thus create that field. See Albert Einstein and
Leopold Infeld, *The Evolution of Physics* (New York, Simon and Schuster,
1938), p. 259.

entity produced by adding its respective parts. It is not valid to fractionate the manufacturing organization or reify observations or measurements. They are simply dimensions of a multidimensional organization.

The various dimensions may be evident through a variety of data.[2] Some of these dimensions may be directly observed. Others may only be inferred. However, each dimension is interrelated with the others, and each has a relative magnitude which is a function of the "whole" of which it is a "part."

Conceptually, the "whole" may be divided into parts, but in order to understand the functioning of "parts" the "whole" must be reconstructed. The formulation of manufacturing problems in terms of two or three variables capable of being studied by statistical methods has limited applicability in providing an understanding of the manufacturing plant's functioning. The measurement of any specific dimension of the plant is significant primarily as it is relative to the other dimensions of that organization.[3]

Thus, wage incentives are only one dimension in a multidimensional environment. Their impact is in part determined by and in part determines the nature of the plant as a whole.

This investigation reveals that wage incentives as a determining force release tendencies toward increased earnings, improved production control, increased intensity of work, grievances over standards of output, grievances over changes in job conditions, slowdowns, ceilings on output, falsification of production reports, decreased effectiveness of lower level supervision, resistance to change, and fric-

[2] For example, see Chap. II, above.

[3] This fact seems to have been overlooked by many of the industrial relations researchers. They concentrate on establishing norms for dimensions ranging from employee satisfaction to the ratio between personnel department workers and total plant employment. The point to be emphasized is that to understand the functioning of any organization it is necessary to study its various dimensions in relation to one another.

tion between and within work groups. The magnitude of these impacts varies from situation to situation.

Environmental forces, such as management leadership, union leadership, labor market competition, product market competition, and the composition of the plant's work force, largely determine the direction and intensity of the impact caused by wage incentives.

Of these determinants, economic forces are of primary importance. Throughout the case studies it was evident that tight labor markets and expanding product markets tend to bring out the diseconomies of wage incentives. Management tends to relax or lose its control of wage incentives. Loose rates, costly grievances, padded allowance times, distorted earnings structures, and severe pressures to extend wage incentives to the entire work force of the plant are the prevailing patterns associated with these conditions.

In a buyer's labor market and/or in keenly competitive product markets, the severity of these activities decreases. Under such conditions, there is a noticeable reduction in the diseconomies of wage incentives. Fewer grievances, adjustment of out-of-line standards, fewer special allowances, increased output, and less resistance to change are the prevalent tendencies. In short, as company profits grow and the power of labor increases, the disadvantages of wage incentives often tend to outweigh their advantages.[4]

4 The most dramatic example of results of expanding markets, ologopolistic competition, and union power occurred in Case 4, a case study of a large steel mill. In this company the most flagrant episodes of restriction of output, loose standards, distorted wage structure, costly strikes, and low morale of lower level supervisors were observed.

In Case 1, postwar reconversion seriously threatened the company's survival. Recognition of this fact caused the union and management to make significant changes in the incentive system. In certain departments wage incentives were abandoned, in others rate cutting was direct and open, and in others the bonus paid to indirect workers was arbitrarily reduced.

In Case 2, the year 1946 found management seriously considering selling its plant. Recognition of the economic pressures giving rise to this con-

It must be emphasized that good management may temper the tendency for high profits and tight labor markets to bring out the worst in wage incentives. However, even in such cases the relative impact of wage incentives changes with changes in the broader economic environment. This was illustrated in Cases 3 and 7.

In Case 3, a plant manufacturing women's undergarments, the company has always maintained a position of leadership in the industry. It has been expanding continually for the past ten years. Employer-employee relations are at a high level. The company maintains one of the most progressive labor policies in the industry. It has successfully resisted the attempts of unions to organize its plant. In this environment wage incentives work reasonably well. However, it is apparent that the efficacy of the wage incentive plan varied with conditions in the labor market. During the Second World War the frictions and rigidities of wage incentives were more frequently encountered.

In Case 7, the management of the company is aware of most of the pitfalls of wage incentives. It has established a firm policy to avoid the disadvantages associated with their use. (For example, it holds that bonus earnings are something "extra"; it refuses to give workers any guarantee that they will earn a bonus; it applies wage incentives to operator-paced work only; it will not grant special allowances to maintain average earnings; it refuses to set standards without thorough motion and time study; and it steadfastly maintains management's prerogative to determine job methods and to set standards.) Despite this policy, it was noticeable that, during the emergency period

---

sideration served to change the attitudes of workers and supervisors. With this change, wage incentives ceased to be the focal point of union agitation. Slowdowns, cheating, strikes, and grievances decreased markedly and the level of worker output increased.

of the Second World War, laxities in the administration
of wage incentives occurred, and increased friction and
agitation followed.

In summary, the importance of wage incentives tends to
be overshadowed by other dimensions of the operating environment. Wage incentives release tendencies toward
economy and diseconomy. Evidence of these tendencies is
clearly observed in all case studies. However, the net effect
of these tendencies is a function of a complex of forces,
such as economic conditions, union leadership, management leadership, and plant morale. Of these, economic conditions are of primary importance. They appear to condition the attitudes and activities of both labor and management.[5]

In the last analysis, the effect of wage incentives is so
dependent on these other factors that it is unrealistic to
think of them as having a significant independent impact
on plant management.

PRECEPTS AND CAVEATS

Despite the dangers of generalizing widely on the administration of wage incentives, this investigation has indicated
that many of the problems encountered are common to
most manufacturing environments. Hence, the following
observations have been framed as precepts and caveats to
guide practitioners in the use of wage incentives. No more
is claimed for them than that they are procedures which

___

[5] For a dramatic account of a change in attitudes and activities see William F. Whyte, *A Pattern for Industrial Peace* (New York, Harper and
Brothers, 1951). Whyte has written a detailed analysis of Case 2 of this
study. Unfortunately, he concentrates on describing the changes in attitudes
and activities without emphasizing that the "pattern" was forged by an economic crisis (the company was considering selling the plant; the workers
had been out on strike for 191 days; the average worker had seven years'
seniority; the plant had a long history of losing money, etc.).

may be useful in avoiding or solving common wage incentive problems.[6]

Wage incentives are most useful in gaining short-run benefits. In the short run, they are one of the most effective devices for increasing workers' output or circumventing wage stabilization. However, over a period of time the benefits gained from their use tend to be offset by the associated costs.[7] These include loosening of standards, friction between workers, grievances over rates, cheating and trickery on the part of workers, and the like.

[6] Most writers on the subject of wage incentives at one time or another draw up a list of principles for "sound" administration. Analysis reveals five common principles: 1. Wage incentives must be fair. 2. They must offer a strong financial incentive. 3. They must be readily understood. 4. They must be based on sound standards of output. 5. They must be separate and distinct from the structure of hourly wage rates.
Unfortunately none of these contributors has, to this writer's knowledge, rigorously analyzed his principles. They all overlook these facts: (1) Criteria for judging fairness may be and often are contradictory. (2) Understanding is a function of mutuality of trust as well as formal communications. (3) There are serious obstacles to the establishment of sound standards of output. Thus, in general, they fail to provide constructive guidance for the administration of wage incentives. See: J. K. Louden, *Wage Incentives* (New York, John Wiley and Sons, Inc., 1944), pp. 16–36, 46–48, E. A. Cyrol, "How to Make an Incentive Plan Work Successfully," in *Job Evaluation and Wage Incentives*, ed. by Carl C. Harrington (New York, Conover-Mast Publications, Inc., 1949), pp. 171–72; War Production Board Memorandum, September, 1943, cited in *Experience of 123 Companies with Wage Incentive Plans, Section I* (Chicago, The Dartnell Corporation, 1944); Charles W. Lytle, *Wage Incentive Methods* (rev. ed.; New York, Ronald Press Co., 1942), pp. 71–73; Lionel B. Michael, *Wage and Salary Fundamentals and Procedures* (New York, McGraw-Hill Book Co., Inc., 1950), pp. 192, 197; Norman C. Hunt, *Methods of Wage Payment in British Industry* (London, Sir Isaac Pitman and Sons, Ltd., 1951), pp. 147–50.
[7] The existence of this tendency has been substantiated by the observations of Wrape, Whyte, Patton, and Roy. H. Edward Wrape, "Tightening Work Standards," *Harvard Business Review*, XXX (July–August, 1952), 64–74; William F. Whyte, "Economic Incentives and Human Relations," *Harvard Business Review*, XXX (March–April, 1952), 73–80; John A. Patton, "What's the Trouble with Wage Incentive Plans?" *Industrial Management Bulletin* (November–December, 1947), p. 19; Don Roy, *How, Why and How Much Do Workers Restrict Output?* (reproduced by the Committee of Human Relations in Industry, University of Chicago, Publication No. 11, July, 1949).

Competent administration of wage incentives starts with the proper choice of the plan to be used. This choice involves consideration of the nature of the work and the present level of operator efficiency.

For relatively effective administration it is best to have wage incentives cover the majority of plant workers. Certainly 85 to 90 percent of the workers should be covered. Unless this is done, incentive earnings automatically result in distortion of the wage structure and associated agitation and friction.

The characteristics of the work may indicate that a group incentive plan is desirable. For example, the need for cooperation, the difficulty in measuring individual output, the possibility of minimizing work in process inventories, and the ease of calculating bonus earnings may indicate that a group plan is most practical. If this is so, every effort should be made to keep the size of the group at a minimum. Otherwise, individual incentive will be diluted and the net impact of the group plan will be reduced.[8]

[8] This study has been concerned primarily with the use of incentives based on the output of individual workers. This focus developed from the fact that, with only two exceptions, the cases investigated revealed an overwhelming rejection of the use of group plans. In most of the plants group plans were used only if it was impractical to set up individual incentive systems. The reasons for this are: (1) Group plans limit management's flexibility. Each change in group composition tends to present problems regarding the breaking in of a new worker. (2) The individual worker's incentive to work is diluted. (3) Group plans tend to engender friction within the group. (4) Group plans tend to weaken management controls, that is, under the group system individual output is not automatically checked.

For one of the most complete studies of group wage incentive systems, see C. C. Balderston, *Group Incentives* (Philadelphia, University of Pennsylvania Press, 1930). Balderston summarizes the advantages of group plans as follows: (1) They are a spur to cooperative effort, not individual self-interest. (2) The social pressure within the group encourages the slackers to increase output, whereas under individual incentives it is argued that pressure is exerted upon the rapid workers to "peg" their production in order to protect the rate. (3) In order to guard the bonus that has already been earned, workers paid in groups voluntarily seek to be transferred or

The choice of a formula for relating worker earnings to output should consider the existing level of worker efficiency and the probability of runaway rates. If the existing level of efficiency is extremely low, a modification of the Rowan or Halsey formulae should be used. This will allow bonus earnings to start at a relatively low level of worker efficiency and thus will help to overcome the resistance that would be met if workers had to perform at the high task level of output prior to earning the bonus. In addition, on a limited amount of relatively unstandardized work, the use of a self-limiting bonus plan may be helpful in allowing both broad coverage of rank-and-file workers and protection against serious distortion in the wage structure.[9]

Carefully plan the installation of the wage incentive system. Work out all of the major administrative policies in advance of installation, and be prepared to install the

---

to be sent home when work is becoming scarce. (4) They offer an inducement to utilize spare time on another operation in the team. When the operations are progressively arranged along a conveyor, the use of spare moments to help out those who are behind tends to keep the operations in balance even when the rate of production varies. (5) They stimulate the training of new employees by fellow workers and the exchange of trade knowledge. (6) In order to increase the group efficiency, workers assist in planning and supervising their own work. (7) "Work-in-process" inventories are reduced because the output must pass the "payment point" to be counted and, therefore, does not stop between operations. (8) The clerical cost of counting work and figuring the payroll is reduced and the quantities paid for can be checked more accurately than when individual incentives are used.

[9] In Cases 1, 15, and 26 such formulae were used with considerable success. For example, in Case 15 the shipping department insisted on an incentive plan to restore traditional earnings differentials in the plant. To end a serious slowdown in that department, management installed a group bonus plan using a modification of the Rowan formula. The relationship of bonus to output was calculated by the following formula:

$$\text{Percent bonus} = \tfrac{1}{2} \left(\frac{\text{Time allowed} - \text{Time taken}}{\text{Time allowed}} \right)$$

Hence, as additional units of time were saved, the workers received a decreasing share of each unit. The maximum bonus that workers could earn was 50 percent. This was only theoretically possible. In order to earn a 50 percent bonus, the work would have to be performed in zero time.

plan as an entity. Avoid piecemeal installation. It tends to generate pressures for hurried work, with the result that the requirements for effective administration are neglected.

Occasionally, to win worker acceptance, it may be desirable to install the plan on a trial basis. In such a case, choose a department in which it appears that the workers will give the greatest positive response to the plan. However, at the same time be ready to install the plan in any or all of the other departments. Thus, if the bonus earnings in the one department lead to pressures for a spread of the system, management will be able to act promptly.

At the outset of the installation of the incentive system, state emphatically that bonus earnings are extra pay for extra work. This policy must be maintained. It means that management will not give special allowances or average earnings for unusual work conditions or if workers are moved to new jobs. If these occur, the worker will be paid his guaranteed hourly rate or his current earnings under the incentive formula, whichever is greater. The management must clearly convey to the workers and the union the fact that incentive earnings can be gained only by increased output.

The need for this policy is obvious. Without it, wage incentives are easily perverted into schemes for increasing workers' earnings without increasing their production, and management may be plagued by numerous requests for special allowances to cover unusual job conditions.

Recognize that the union is essentially a political body. Hence, do not expect it to act in a manner that conflicts with the political needs of its officers. Attempt to minimize the possible union pressure for loose standards of performance by keeping bonus earnings "extra," and by avoiding negotiation of the details of the system.

In the labor-management agreement, attempt to secure

clauses that: (1) Recognize management's right to determine methods and standards of performance. (2) Allow the union to challenge standards under the established grievance procedure. (3) Provide for the arbitration of grievances over standards by an impartial industrial engineer. The arbitration clause should provide that the company and the union share the expense of arbitration equally. (4) Outlaw wildcat strikes and slowdowns. The no-strike, no-slowdown clause should recognize management's right to discipline offenders. (5) Recognize bonuses as being distinct and separate from the structure of hourly wages. This clause should concisely and simply state that the company makes no guarantee of bonus earnings or incentive work.

It is important not to state formally the incentive factor allowed under the plan. The reason for this may be illustrated by a simple example. If the company states in its labor-management agreement that incentive rates will be set to allow the average operator to earn 25 percent bonus for average productivity, the workers have a benchmark for arguing that a given standard is too tight. They will restrict production, and unless management can prove the existence of the slowdown, the workers will have a case for relaxing the standard.

Guard against the wage incentive plan's undermining the authority and responsibility of the foreman. One of the prevailing tendencies in the use of wage incentives is for the industrial engineers to take over many of the foreman's functions. The foreman becomes subjected to so many checks and investigations that he hesitates to decide and act on many everyday problems.[10]

For the wage incentive system to function efficiently,

[10] For a general analysis of this tendency, see Douglas McGregor, "The Staff Function in Human Relations," *The Journal of Social Issues,* IV (Summer, 1948), 5–22.

the foreman's role as an important link in the chain of line authority must be maintained. The foreman must be relied upon to assume the major functions involved in supervising his department.

Since the foreman is actually responsible for the administration of the wage incentive system, his willing cooperation must be forthcoming. This may best be achieved by consultations prior to the installation of the wage incentive system. Discussions should center around the benefits that may accrue and the problems that will be encountered. The general principle to follow is that the foreman should be asked to express his opinion before top management decides to act.

Once the decision to install wage incentives has been made, the foreman must be educated to administer the system properly. His education should provide an understanding of the procedure for setting standards and the problems that arise in day-to-day activities.

One of the best techniques for educating the foreman is to use case materials drawn from actual plant situations. These cases should first be studied by the foremen and then should be thoroughly discussed in a general foremen's meeting. On the basis of the discussions, a foreman's manual should be developed. This manual should describe and explain the policy to be followed in handling the more common problems of wage incentive administration.

Use complete and thorough motion and time study in setting performance standards. If time study is to be used intelligently, its inherent weaknesses must be recognized. Furthermore, management must be willing to incur short-run losses in order to insure that standards are based on adequate studies.

Where feasible, standard data should be developed and used as a basis for rate setting. Every effort should be made to gain worker acceptance of standard data as a device for rate setting. Its use will reduce administrative costs and tend to insure greater consistency between standards.

Install the standard in a manner that will avoid making an issue of the new rate. This may be accomplished by first assigning the newly rated job to a worker who has a reputation for giving new standards a reasonable trial. Another practice that may aid in gaining acceptance of rates is to avoid an elaborate ceremony for announcing a new rate. Simply state the rate on the worker's job ticket; don't send copies of it to the union or post it on the bulletin board.[11]

Handle grievances over rates in a nonlegalistic manner. Avoid arguing the soundness of the time study technique. Simply recognize the possibility of honest disagreement and restudy the job. Before restudying the job, make certain that the foreman is completely aware of the facts. Have him observe the work while the new study is being made. His role is to insure that proper work methods are used and to pass judgment on the standard. At the time of the new study, have the department's union steward observe the operation. Call his attention to any avoidable delays or other conditions that should be discounted.

To facilitate the handling of grievances, take motion pictures of all short-cycle jobs. In a corner of the picture include a large time study clock. This procedure will provide an objective and relatively tangible means for dealing with disputes over standards or methods of performance.

Recognize that a poor system for collecting time or productivity data encourages workers to falsify records.[12]

[11] It should be understood that, when this procedure is followed, the workers and the union may request copies of time studies and other pertinent information explaining the basis for the new rate.

[12] The use of the lie detector has shown that: "No man is altogether honest or altogether dishonest, any more than he is altogether industrious or altogether lazy. Under ordinary conditions, most of us are fairly

Hence, at the outset of the installation carefully establish a thorough system of cross checks and procedures to minimize the possibility of workers cheating.

Guarantee each standard for only a limited period of time (such as six months) and review standards periodically to keep them up to date. This recommendation stems from the fact that the workers need a guarantee against rate cuts. The usual guarantee given by management is that standards apply to a given method, and, therefore, as long as the method for performing the work remains unchanged, the standard is to apply. This guarantee is quite meaningless. If workers' earnings are exceptionally high, management designs a new method as an excuse for tightening the standard. One study points out that "this procedure may be repeated many times and serves to emphasize the fact that there is a potential method change on almost every operation." [13]

The practice of guaranteeing standards for a specified time period frankly and openly recognizes that market pressures may force management to adjust rates. Furthermore, it may encourage workers to apply their special knowledge of the job to improve methods. The fear of immediate rate cuts will be removed. The only condition justifying a change in a standard prior to the expiration of the time period for which it is guaranteed should be a significant change in method initiated by management. The working definition of "significant" must be expressed to insure that minor job changes will not be used as an excuse for rate cuts. For example, it may be defined to

honest and fairly industrious. Under favorable conditions, most of us may become scrupulously honest and amazingly industrious, or vice versa." Walter Dill Scott, Robert C. Clothier, and William R. Spriegel, *Personnel Management* (4th ed.; New York, McGraw-Hill Book Co., Inc., 1949), p. 279.

[13] National Industrial Conference Board, *Some Problems in Wage Incentive Administration*, No. 19 in *Studies in Personnel Policy*, (February, 1940), p. 12.

indicate that the change in method must result in an increase in output of better than 35 percent.

Recognize that rank-and-file workers tend to resist method changes and job transfers. This resistance arises from fear of economic loss, fear of being unable to reach a former level of efficiency, and a general fear of the unknown. Wherever feasible, attempt to minimize these fears by timing the installation of methods improvements during periods of expanding employment, carefully training the workers in the new methods, and consulting with the workers in advance of the change.

Conclusion

There is nearly universal agreement with the moral propositions of wage incentives. However, their administration is clouded with conflict. This arises from the following limitations inherent in the technique.

Precise standards of performance cannot be established. Machines, men, and raw materials may vary from day to day and from hour to hour. It is practically impossible to standardize job conditions completely. Even if jobs could be standardized, there would be room for considerable debate as to "correct" standards. Weaknesses in the technique of time study (such as human errors in reading the stopwatch, in leveling, and in determining fatigue and delay allowances) prevent the determination of consistent standards of performance.

The use of a system of payment by results sharpens and accentuates differences between the goals of management and those of workers. The theory underlying the use of wage incentives holds that a system of payment by results puts men into business for themselves and that, in pursuing their own self-interest, workers will increase their rate of output. Therefore, it is reasoned, wage incentives provide a technique for stimulating increased production by enabling workers to increase their earnings. The weakness of this logic arises from the fact that the worker's self-interest not only prompts him to increase output but also encourages him to fight for lenient standards of output. With wage incentives, differences of opinion as to appropriate standards of output and proper allowances for variations in job conditions are translated directly into money income.

Wage incentives tend to distort traditional wage structures. The use of a system of payment by results injects a dynamic element into the wage structure. Traditional wage differentials are often upset. From the workers' point of view such changes frequently appear illogical and unreasonable. This distortion of the wage structure is inherent in the use of systems of payment by result in remunerating rank-and-file factory workers. It arises out of (1) differences in potential earnings on different jobs, (2) differences in ability among workers on the same job; (3) differences in the ability of a specific worker on different jobs, and (4) differences in the pressures that groups of workers may apply for loosening up standards of output.

In the last analysis it must be recognized that, although wage incentives may be useful in plant management, they have inherent weaknesses leading to rigidities, friction, and hypertrophy. Hence, the best approach to the problem of whether or not to use wage incentives is to begin with the assumption that they are not needed and then carefully examine the pros and cons of their use. If net benefits may be attained, then proceed to install the appropriate plan. But recognize that wage incentives may be given credit for results that might have been gained more readily by independent means. For example, wage incentives are not required in order to set realistic standards of performance, to standardize job conditions, to improve methods of work, to compare individual performance against standard performance, or to improve personnel management.

In short, wage incentives are often credited with results that properly belong elsewhere. The decision to install wage incentives must avoid this confusion.

Bibliography

UNPUBLISHED MATERIALS

McGregor, Douglas. "The Supervisor's Job." Address before the Management Forum, E. I. du Pont de Nemours and Co., Inc., Wilmington, Delaware, April 16, 1948.
Whisler, T. L. Merit Rating: A Management Tool. Unpublished Ph.D. dissertation, School of Business, University of Chicago, 1953.

PUBLIC DOCUMENTS

United States Department of Labor, Bureau of Labor Statistics. Agreement Provisions. Bulletin No. 686. Washington, U.S. Government Printing Office, 1942.
—— Effect of Incentive Payments on Hourly Earnings. Bulletin No. 742. Washington, U.S. Government Printing Office, 1943.
—— Incentive Wage Plans and Collective Bargaining. Bulletin No. 717. Washington, U.S. Government Printing Office, 1942.
—— Incentive Wage Provisions. Preliminary draft, April, 1947.
—— Time Studies and Standards of Production. Preliminary draft, June, 1947.
—— Wage Structure: Radios, 1947. Series 2, No. 2 Washington, U.S. Government Printing Office, 1948.
United States War Production Board. Addresses and Papers on Wage Incentive Plans and Labor Management Relationships. Vol. IV (1944). Mimeographed.

OTHER PUBLISHED WORKS

Abruzzi, Adam. Work Measurement. New York, Columbia University Press, 1952.

Alford, L. P., ed. Management's Handbook. New York, Ronald Press Co., 1923.

Alford, L. P., and John R. Bangs, eds. Production Handbook. New York, Ronald Press Co., 1944.

American Machinist, January 3, 1946, pp. 97–108.

Bakke, E. Wight. The Unemployed Worker. New Haven, Yale University Press, 1940.

Balderston, C. C. Group Incentives. Philadelphia, University of Pennsylvania Press, 1930.

Barnard, Chester I. The Functions of the Executive. Cambridge, Mass., Harvard University Press, 1938.

Barnes, Ralph. Motion and Time Study. 2d ed. New York, John Wiley and Sons, 1940.

Bloomfield, Daniel. Financial Incentives for Employees and Executives. Vol. I. New York, The H. W. Wilson Co., 1923.

Blum, M. L., and J. J. Russ. "A Study of Employee Attitudes toward Various Incentives," *Personnel,* XIX (1942), 438–44.

Brech, E. F. L. The Nature and Significance of Management. 2d ed. London, Sir Isaac Pitman and Sons, Ltd., 1948.

Brown, W. B. D. "Incentives within the Factory," *Occupational Psychology,* XIX, No. 2 (April, 1945), 82.

Bureau of National Affairs, Inc. Basic Patterns in Collective Bargaining Contracts. Washington, 1949.

Carrol, Phil, Jr. Time Study for Cost Control. New York, McGraw-Hill Book Co., Inc., 1943.

Chamberlain, Neil W. The Union Challenge to Management Control. New York, Harper and Brothers, 1948.

Cole, G. D. H. The Payment of Wages. London, George Allen and Unwin, Ltd., 1918.

Collins, Orvis, Melville Dalton, and Donald Roy. "Restriction of Output and Social Cleavage in Industry," *Applied Anthropology,* V, No. 3 (Summer, 1946), 1–14.

Commons, John R., ed. Trade Unionism and Labor Problems. New York, Ginn and Co., 1921.

Dalton, Melville. "The Industrial Rate-Buster: A Characterization," *Applied Anthropology,* VII, No. 1 (Winter, 1948), 5–18.

—— "Worker Response and Social Background," *The Journal of Political Economy*, LV (August, 1947), 323–32.

Dartnell Corporation. Experience of 117 Companies with Wage Incentive Plans. Chicago, 1948.

—— Experience of 123 Companies with Wage Incentive Plans, Sections I and II. Chicago, 1944.

Davis, Allison. "The Motivation of the Underprivileged Worker," in William F. Whyte, ed., Industry and Society. New York, McGraw-Hill Book Co., Inc., 1946.

Davis, Norah. "Some Psychological Effects on Women Workers of Payment by the Individual Bonus Method," *Occupational Psychology*, XVIII, No. 2 (April, 1944), 53–62.

Dean, Joel. Managerial Economics. New York, Prentice-Hall, Inc., 1951.

Diemer, Hugo, ed. Wage-Payment Plans That Reduce Production Costs. New York, McGraw-Hill Publishing Co., Inc., 1929.

Einstein, Albert, and Leopold Infeld. The Evolution of Physics. New York, Simon and Schuster, 1938.

Factory Management and Maintenance, February, 1948.

Forbes, W. D. "Why Piece-Work Is Not Satisfactory," *American Machinist*, LII (March 18, 1920), 612.

Friend, J. G., and Ernest A. Haggard. Work Adjustment in Relation to Family Background: A Conceptual Basis for Counseling. Stanford, Stanford University Press, 1948.

Gardner, Burleigh, and David Moore. Human Relations in Industry. Rev. ed. Chicago, Richard D. Irwin, Inc., 1950.

Gilman, Nicholas P. Profit Sharing Between Employer and Employee. New York, Houghton, Mifflin and Co., 1889.

Going, Charles B. Principles of Industrial Engineering. New York, McGraw-Hill Book Co., Inc., 1911.

Golden, C., and H. Ruttenberg. The Dynamics of Industrial Democracy. New York, Harper and Brothers, 1942.

Gomberg, William. A Trade Union Analysis of Time Study. Chicago, Science Research Associates, 1948.

Halsey, F. A. "The Premium Plan of Paying for Labor," in Transactions of the American Society of Mechanical Engineers, Vol. XII.

Harbison, Frederick H., and Robert Dubin. Patterns of Union-Management Relations. Chicago, Science Research Associates, 1947.

Harrington, Carl C., ed. Job Evaluation and Wage Incentives. New York, Conover-Mast Publications, Inc., 1949.

Hersey, R. B. "Psychology of Workers," Personnel Journal, XIV (1936), 291–96.

Hoppock, R., and S. Spiegler. "Job Satisfaction," Occupations, The Vocational Guidance Magazine, XVI (1938), 636–43.

Hoslett, S. D., ed. Human Factors in Management. Rev. ed. New York, Harper and Brothers, 1951.

Hoxie, Robert F. Scientific Management and Labor. New York, D. Appleton and Co., 1915.

Hunt, Norman C. Methods of Wage Payment in British Industry. London, Sir Isaac Pitman and Sons, Ltd., 1951.

Industrial Management, LVII (June, 1919), 470–72.

International Labour Office. Payment by Results. Geneva, 1951.

Jurgensen, Clifford. "Selected Factors Which Influence Job Performance," Journal of Applied Psychology, XXXI (1937), 553–64.

Kennedy, Van Dusen. Union Policy and Incentive Wage Methods. New York, Columbia University Press, 1945.

Lindahl, Lawrence G. "What Makes a Good Job?" Personnel, XXV (1949), 263–66.

Livernash, E. Robert. "Stabilization of the Internal Wage Rate Structure," Industrial and Labor Relations Review, Vol. VII, No. 2 (January, 1954).

Louden, J. K. Wage Incentives. New York, John Wiley and Sons, Inc., 1944.

Lytle, Charles W. Wage Incentive Methods. Rev. ed. New York, Ronald Press Co., 1938.

McCabe, David A. "The Standard Rate in American Trade Unions," in Johns Hopkins University Studies in Historical and Political Science, Series XXI, No. 2. Baltimore, The Johns Hopkins Press, 1912.

Mace, C. A. Incentives: Some Experimental Studies. Industrial Health Research Board, Report No. 72. Great Britain, 1935.

McGregor, Douglas. "The Staff Function in Human Relations," *The Journal of Social Issues,* IV, No. 3 (Summer, 1948), 5–22.

Malaurin, Rupert W., and Charles A. Myers. "Wages and the Movement of Factory Labor," *The Quarterly Journal of Economics,* LVII (February, 1943), 241–64.

Management Review, Vol. XXXVII (October, 1948), Vol. XXXVIII (January, 1949).

Marx, Karl. Capital. Modern Library ed. New York, Random House, Inc., 1906.

Mathewson, Stanley. Restriction of Output among Unorganized Workers. New York, Viking Press, 1931.

Mayo, Elton. The Social Problems of an Industrial Civilization. Boston, Harvard University Press, 1945.

Michael, Lionel B. Wage and Salary Fundamentals and Procedures. New York, McGraw-Hill Book Co., Inc., 1950.

Mundel, M. Systematic Time and Motion Study. New York, Prentice-Hall, Inc., 1947.

Myers, Charles A., and George P. Shultz. The Dynamics of a Labor Market. New York, Prentice-Hall, Inc., 1951.

National Industrial Conference Board, Inc. Factors Affecting Employee Morale. No. 85 in Studies in Personnel Policy. New York, 1947.

—— Some Problems in Wage Incentive Administration. No. 19 in Studies in Personnel Policy. New York, 1940.

—— Systems of Wage Payment. New York, 1930.

—— Wage Incentive Practices. No. 68 in Studies in Personnel Policy. New York, 1945.

Patton, John A. "What's the Trouble with Wage Incentive Plans?" *Industrial Management Bulletin,* November–December, 1947.

Perrin, F. A. C. "An Experimental Study of Motor Ability," *Journal of Experimental Psychology,* IV (1927), 24–56.

Person, Harlow S. "Methods of Remuneration," in *Encyclopedia of the Social Sciences.* 1935 ed., Vol. VIII.

Pigors, P., and C. Myers. Personnel Administration. 2d ed. New York, McGraw-Hill Book Co., Inc., 1950.

Presgrave, Ralph. The Dynamics of Time Study. 2d ed. New York, McGraw-Hill Book Co., Inc., 1945.

Reynolds, Lloyd George. The Structure of Labor Markets. New York, Harper and Brothers, 1951.

Reynolds, Lloyd George, and Joseph Shister. Job Horizons. New York, Harper and Brothers, 1948.

Riegel, John W. "Essentials in Incentive Compensation," in Development in Wage Payment Techniques, American Management Association Personnel Series, No. 77 (1944), pp. 11–22.

Roethlisberger, F. J., and W. J. Dickson. Management and the Worker. Cambridge, Mass., Harvard University Press, 1939.

Roy, Don. How, Why and How Much Do Workers Restrict Output? Chicago, Committee of Human Relations in Industry, University of Chicago, 1949.

Sayles, Leonard R. "The Impact of Incentives on Inter-Group Work Relations: A Management and Union Problem," *Personnel*, May, 1952, pp. 483–90.

Schloss, David F. Methods of Industrial Remuneration. 3d ed. Oxford, England, Williams and Norgate, 1898.

Scott, Walter Dill, Robert C. Clothier, and William R. Spriegel. Personnel Management. 4th ed. New York, McGraw-Hill Book Co., Inc., 1949.

Selekman, Benjamin. "Living with Collective Bargaining," *Harvard Business Review*, Vol. XX, 1941.

Shaffer, L. F. Psychology of Adjustment. Boston, Houghton Mifflin Co., 1936.

Sherman, Joseph M. "Incentive Pay in American Industry, 1945–1946," *Monthly Labor Review*, LXV (1947), 535–38.

Slichter, Sumner H. Union Policies and Industrial Management. Washington, Brookings Institution, 1941.

Smith, Adam. Wealth of Nations. Modern Library ed. New York, Random House, Inc., 1937.

Stearns, W. D. "Wage Payment Systems in Machine Shops," *Machinery*, XXV (August, 1919), 1115–16.

Steel Case Research Committee of the Steel Industry. Steel Wages, A National Issue, 1944.

Tannenbaum, Robert. "The Managerial Concept: A Rational Synthesis," *The Journal of Business*, XXII (October, 1949), 225–40.

Taylor, F. W. "A Piece-Rate System," in Transactions of the American Society of Mechanical Engineers, XVI (1895), 856–903.

Thomson, W. Rowan. The Premium Bonus System. Glasgow, Scotland, McCorquodale and Co., Ltd., 1917.

Towne, Henry R. "Gain Sharing," in Transactions of the American Society of Mechanical Engineers, Vol. X, 1889.

Uhrbrock, R. S. A Psychologist Looks at Wage Incentive Methods. New York, American Management Association, 1935.

Webb, Sidney, and Beatrice Webb. Industrial Democracy. London, Longmans, Green and Co., 1902.

Whyte, William F. "Economic Incentives and Human Relations," Harvard Business Review, XXX, No. 2 (March–April, 1952), 73–80.

—— "Incentives for Productivity: The Bundy Tubing Case," Applied Anthropology, Vol. VII, Spring, 1948.

—— A Pattern for Industrial Peace. New York, Harper and Brothers, 1951.

Wolf, R. B. "Nonfinancial Incentives," in Publications of the American Society of Mechanical Engineers, No. 1673 (1918).

Wrape, H. Edward. "Tightening Work Standards," Harvard Business Review, XXX, No. 4 (July–August, 1952), 64–72.

Young, Kimbal. An Introduction to Sociology. 2d ed. New York, The American Book Co., 1949.

Index

Abruzzi, Adam, 84
Accounting procedures associated with wage incentives: accuracy of records, 66-67; payroll accounting, 70; controls needed, 125-26
Administrative staff, 70
Alford, L. P., 4, 11
Allowances, petitions for special, 37; downtime, 46-47; impact on earnings, 64; suggested policy on, 122
Arbitration clause, need for, 61; example, 61-62
Arbitration of standards, 60-62; suggested policy on, 123
Attitudes, *see under* Foremen; Workers' attitudes

Bakke, E. Wight, 103
Balderston, C. C., 120
Bangs, John R., 11
Banking of output to avoid rate cuts, 45
Barnard, Chester I., 74
Barnes, Ralph, quoted, 82
Bedaux Point Premium Plan, 13-14
Bloomfield, Daniel, 4
Blum, M. L., 104
Bonus, defined, 6; example, 23
Bonus earnings, suggested policy, 122
Brech, E. F. L., 74
Brown, W. B. D., 89
Bureau of National Affairs, quoted, 52-53

Carrol, Phil, Jr., quoted, 81-82
Ceilings on output, compared with the slowdown, 40-41; identifying ceilings, 41-42; establishing ceilings, 42-43; policing of, 43; cost of, 44-45; and banking output, 45; and fraudulent records, 45-47; management action to maintain ceilings, 65; in relation to scheduling, 101-3

Chamberlain, Neil W., 74
Change, handling resistance to, 127
Clothier, Robert C., 126
Cole, G. D. H., 3
Collins, Orvis, 40, 41, 89
Commons, John R., 9
Cyrol, E. A., 119

Dalton, Melville, 40, 41, 89
Davis, Allison, 89
Davis, Norah, 90
Day work, 5n
Dean, Joel, 74
Dennison, Henry, 25
Department of Labor, Bureau of Labor Statistics: study of impact of wage incentives on hourly earnings, 22-23; study of collective bargaining clauses related to wage incentives, 53
Dickson, William J., 41, 45
Diemer, Hugo, 4, 11
Dubin, Robert, 31, 62; quoted, 63
Dyer plan, 14

Economic forces, role of, in determining the impact of wage incentives, 116
Economics, assumptions of implicit in wage incentives, 91-93
Einstein, Albert, 114
Emerson, Harrington, 24

Forbes, W. D., 24
Foremen, instructions received by, 53-56; attitudes toward wage incentives, 111-13; problems of, under wage incentives, 123-24
Fraudulent practices, in relation to ceilings on output, 45-47; action by management to prevent, 66-67; precept for avoiding, 125-26
Friend, J. G., 89

Gantt Task and Bonus System, 15
Gardner, Burleigh, 41

95-96; impact of, on work methods, 96-99; impact of, on planning and scheduling, 99-103; impact on recruitment, selection, placement, and training, 103-7; impact on personnel management, 103-13; impact of, on cooperative relations in the plant, 108-13; importance of, in plant management, 114-18; precepts and caveats for the use of, 118-27; choosing a plan, 120-21; group incentives, 120-21; installing a wage incentive system, 121-22; inherent weaknesses of, 127-29

Wages: maintaining an acceptable wage structure, 30-48; problems arising from distortion of the wage structure, 32-40, 108-9, 115; management actions to preserve the wage structure, 62-66; as a device for attracting labor, 103-6; as a device for holding labor, 104-5; earnings under wage incentives during the Second World War, 105-6

Wage stabilization, wage incentives as a device for evading regulations of, 68, 105, 119

Wage structure, *see under* Wages

War Production Board, 23, 119

Webb, Sidney, and Beatrice Webb, 3, 8

Whisler, T. L., 106

Whyte, William F., 89, 95, 118, 119

Wolf, R. B., 9

Work assignments, impact of wage incentives on, 65

Workers' attitudes: toward standards of performance, 35-37; toward fellow workers, 38-40; toward rate busters, 40

Work Factor, 58

Wrape, H. Edward, 119

Young, Kimbal, 86